WRITE LIKE YOU'RE ALREA

M LeMont & Jennifer C. Lopez

"There Is No Exquisite Beauty Without Some Strangeness." ~E. A. Poe

Welcome

I've been waiting–on you. What took you so long? That's okay, don't answer, I better get busy and tell you a few things–because we don't have a lot of time.

M LeMont, author of the Bestseller How to Gain 100,000 Twitter Followers has released another brilliant book–the sequel, Write Like You're Already Famous, coauthor Jennifer C. Lopez.

One beta reader made a great point. She said this book reminded her of Kim Kardashian–who made herself famous:

"People think *it was the scandalous sex tapes, or her father who represented OJ Simpson that brought her fame. But, Kim had a DIFFERENT MINDSET and made herself famous before she became famous. She also made the Kardashian family famous*."

That success mentality is what this book is all about. It will show you how to THINK DIFFERENTLY and how to Write Like You're Already Famous.

THE BOOK WILL TURN THE LITERARY WORLD UPSIDE DOWN. ~ Buzzmaster

- *ALLURING*
- *INFORMATIVE*
- *FASCINATING*
- *CAPTIVATING*
- *FROTHY*

If you want a deep dive into creative writing, self publishing and marketing secrets then this book will rock your world. ~ Pam Morgan

Dedication

"I'm always thinking of you. When the sun comes up to light the morning skies–when the night moves in and I'm forced to close my eyes–I can't stop thinking of you." ~Victor Fields

Epic2316 that beautiful moment in time that you'll never forget.

Warning:

This book is about the FREEDOM to totally express yourself with a little bit of fear.

If you want to be ordinary, then this book is not for you. It doesn't take much to be ordinary–just be like everybody else; write like everybody else, think like everybody else, and play it safe like everybody else.

Parts of this book are written in 2nd person POV and may be offensive to some readers; but for those of you who are brave at heart, it contains a wealth of information on creative writing, self-publishing, and marketing, that you can't find any place else.

If you are uncomfortable with going against the grain and learning new ideas, then please don't waste your money on buying this book. There are other books more suitable for your taste.

Thank you so much for understanding and having a kind heart.

About the Book Cover

"*One picture is worth 1,000 words.*"

A new generation of fearless writers has emerged and are willing to go beyond traditional norms and practices, blaze new trails. We refer to them as the Think Different Crowd (TDC) If that's you, then keep reading–you came to the right place.

The cover and the title, Write Like You're Already Famous–is a radical view of what it means to stand out from the rest. The woman–wearing a hat, and red lipstick, holding a cigar, with an arrogant stare is an image to evoke strength and depict an attitude of the new wave of creative writers.

What You Can Expect From This Book

This book is a beautiful mess of contradictions, essays, teachings, and strategies on topics that took years to master. It goes against the status quo and is packed with powerful ideas on writing, publishing and marketing. There are 118 essays filled with never before published secrets. Plus, a personal interview with M LeMont is included, one of the most dynamic writers/marketers on the Internet.

The book is carefully written and designed to break down the psychological barriers and constraints that prevent you from becoming a successful writer and marketer.

I DARE YOU to read this book, use it as a guide and tell us that you still THINK in the same way.

I want you to Call Us Out in public if this book doesn't POUND your head with a WEALTH of IDEAS that will make you a better Writer, Self-Publisher, and Marketer.

Can you do that?

If you want to take your writing career to a HIGHER PLANE–accept our product challenge.

@mistersalesman @thejennieration

We look forward to hearing from you.

Table Of Contents

It's Only After You've Lost Everything That You're Free To Do Anything.
Favor & Reciprocity? Ask Me Anything
Own It!
A Quote Can Make it Simple & Easy
Goolge Plus 25K Can I Make Money
You Have To Know What You've Got
What I Learned From Albert Einstein Over Dinner
Reading Time: 2min 2sec
I Want To Ask You A Bunch of Questions!
Nothing Is Impossible For A Man, Who Refuses To Listen To Reason ~Gary Halbert
Do I Need To Treat All My Followers The Same Way?
I Am Thankful For All Who Said No To Me
What's your name?
Negative People. Have No Fear.
"Don't Eat The Cake Elli Mae."
How to gain more followers by hanging dirty laundry on a clothesline
The UNFORGIVING...Who are they?
You came out of NOWHERE...
When You Hit Rock Bottom, it's Time to Celebrate.
Can You Handle The Truth?
To Thyself Be True–Lucky Breaks
How Do I Become Visible on Twitter?
Launch Day
You'll Never Become A Great Writer If You Give Up

Introduction

Whenever you find yourself on the side of the majority, it is time to pause and reflect.

~Mark Twain

M LeMont is proof that going against the grain works. He has published seven books and has over 200,000 Twitter followers.

He published invaluable secrets in the bestseller titled, How To Gain 100,000 Twitter Followers, Secrets Revealed By An Expert. He is also the founder of the wildly popular Retweet Train @mistersalesman on Twitter.

Jennifer C. Lopez is a Spanish Educator, Interpreter & Translator, with an M.A. Ed. She's also a writer and brilliant storyteller.

In this book, Jen and I collaborate. She takes on the awesome challenge of an interview with M LeMont at the fabulous Venetian Hotel in Macao. This premier interview is a rare opportunity packed with high-quality information that will give you an unfair advantage over the competition.

Most authors write to be famous and never succeed because they play it safe. But what they should be doing is writing...like they are already famous.

Did you get that? Let me repeat it and put it in italics.

Don't Write To Be Famous, Write Like You're Already Famous.

There's a certain confidence that comes with this type of thinking. It's like when a reporter once asked Mike Tyson what happens if Plan A doesn't work?

What's your Plan B? Mike said, "There is no Plan B. The idea is, you get it right the first time."

Now that's the attitude you want when you're writing. Hip-hop calls it, 'Swagger.' Flamenco calls it, 'El Ritmo Sabroso'

Confidence Is Not 'They Will Like Me.' Confidence Is 'I'll Be Fine If They Don't.'

Imagine what you could accomplish if you had no fear of rules, rejection, criticism, or specific results.

You would be free of the shackles that have held you back all these years. I bet you feel freer already, don't you? Well, that's good, but first you must learn how to **THINK**.

We designed this book to make you think differently–we pushed the boundaries; two co-authors, two narrators, storytelling, how-to wrapped around a narrative for a lively presentation with powerful marketing tools and secrets.

Throughout this book, there are always two voices talking even though you may think you only hear one. Jennifer and my voice are woven into every word, no matter who's talking.

Okay, are you ready to partake?

******

The book opens with Jennifer C. Lopez going to meet M LeMont for the first time for a rare interview over in Macao, off the coast of Hong Kong. Why now? and why Macao? Well, I'll let Jennifer tell you in her own words.

Chapter 1 Jennifer Lopez: The Ride to First Encounter

I had never been in a private jet. Not even a desire of mine. Guess I'm just not that kinda girl. Simplicity is beautiful to me, not the overly lavish. I've seen what it can do to people.

But nonetheless, here I am, flying on the directives of M LeMont to one of the most beautiful places in the world to meet him for the interview.

It's a rare interview that he hasn't given to anybody else. Why, me? And also what made him decide to co-author the book with me?

Well, it's really too long of a story to tell here on the plane, so I included it in the second half of the book with a few other goodies for you, along with a peek at a chapter from M LeMont's Bestseller, How To Gain 100,000 Twitter Followers.

This interview will give me an opportunity to learn from one of the best Internet marketers, and I'm going to pass the information on to you, my readers. Of course, I had to get his permission to do so.

He also included a lot of his Golden Nuggets that are priceless in the second part of the book.

I told him it's like receiving the rare "Golden Ticket" in Willie Wonka & The Chocolate Factory; the knowledge gained from this golden ticket has more value than a lifetime of chocolates.

I've written down a list of questions and I can share 6 of them with you right now, so tell me what you think?

And please, don't tell me you already know the answers because I can assure you, they may seem common questions, but the answers M LeMont gives–you've never heard before.

Oh my goodness, hold on a sec! Whooo, the jet is swaying a bit too much for my comfort. I see the flight attendant, thank goodness.

Well, such a very debonair gentleman wearing a tux. He sees my look of fear.

Flight Attendant: "Un poquito turbulancia Señora, pero todo bien, solo el aire porque estamos sobre el oceano."

(A little turbulence, but it's all ok, simply air pockets as we are over the ocean.)

I look at him, studying his face and suddenly wondering how he knew I spoke Spanish. Besides, we are on a flight headed to Macao. So, I ask him: "Desculpeme Señor, ¿Es Usted Español, pues de España?" (Excuse me Sir, are you a native Spaniard?)

Flight Attendant: Yes Ms., I am from the southern region of Spain, called Andalucia.

Jennifer: Oh that makes perfect sense. I can tell from your beautiful accent, I used to live there.

Flight Attendant: Yes, M LeMont told me you did. That's why I wanted to speak with you in Spanish.

I smile inside, knowing how typical this is of M LeMont. He thinks of the little details to show he cares, and notices.

Flight Attendant: Might you enjoy a glass of champagne–Dom Perignon we have on ice for you?

Jennifer: Dom Perignon–expensive taste that M LeMont. Definitely and please with a lot of fresh lime. Thank you. And, what is your name?

Flight Attendant: "Me llamo Carlos" (I am Carlos) …smiling (Walks away)

Okay, I'm sorry for the interruption, but I'm glad Carlos came over at that moment. I was gripping the arm of this soft caramel leather recliner so hard because of that turbulence. If it were a person's arm, they might be badly bruised at this point. So, I needed to get my drink refilled and calm these nerves. I'm deathly scared of flying.

I was surprised when boarding the plane that the pilot and copilot were females–now before you say anything, I'm for equal rights and women are just as capable of flying a jet as men.

Anyway, the plane is rolling smoothly across the skies now and I am appreciating the beautiful low-lit surroundings and the gorgeous yellow roses–a symbol of friendship, on the little table at my side.

…every detail, I think again…smiling. I have to be sure my interview with M LeMont is as thorough.

Ok, better get back to telling you a little about what I plan to ask him tonight. Here are a few of the questions, let me know what you think.

1. What are the secrets to selling on the Internet? And please, don't bullshit me because I didn't come all the way to Macao to hear the same old stuff. I want to know how to monetize my Twitter account. I promise this is not going to be your typical, boring interview. You know, the kind that makes you yawn, stretch your arms and pick up another book?

2. Why are people who I interact with not buying my books, even after they click on my book link? I've tried everything and nothing works. What am I doing wrong?

3. What are three critical publishing secrets about Amazon we need to know?

4. Give us the Hashtag secrets? I see that you use as many as 7 when everyone else is using 2.

5. What is the advantage to writing a blog post every day vs. every week? How can I make money?

6. How can I spend less time on Twitter and still be effective?

Now I'm also going to ask him some more personal questions too. He knows I wouldn't be coming here without getting to the heart of a separate but equally important issue.

Yea, it's about him. Who is M LeMont? Why do I care? Why do we care?

I'll tell you right now. Everything that my questions involve relates back to who he is in some way.

He has the most unique marketing technique on the Internet and it is the very reason I wanted to do this interview to begin with. He has answers we writers NEED. His success, effectiveness, even the words and images he uses–they all attract and repel at the same time.

They have brought him undeniable success. And one thing is for sure–M LeMont is not afraid to share his knowledge.

I am certain though–he is going to be pretty 'evasivo' (evasive) on some of this because he is a private man. But, growing to know him from his writings, I believe he is also an honest man and I will be unrelenting here, that I promise you.

No matter what, this interview meeting is going to blow the roof off the word 'conventional.' (laughing)

So, the whole Bobbie Dixon, woman thing and why he has "her" picture on his profile, the Twitter handle @mistersalesman that is clearly a contradiction?

Is it a branding thing to get more attention or a trick to deceive?–Yea, M LeMont may think he's the cat and I'm the mouse, but I'm going to nail this interview.

It is a once in a lifetime opportunity, like interviewing Donald Trump, (boy I would get a kick out that one) and I plan on walking away with as much business information as I can.

Okay, I'm going to hit the button on this comfy leather recliner and take a real cat’s nap.

Oh, I wish you could see what I am seeing out this window right now. The snow covered mountains and the orange tipped clouds– simply breathtaking.

I hope when I awaken we'll be landing in Macao. Bye for now.

Chapter 2 Arrival In Macao

"Hello, M LeMont this is Jennifer I've arrived here in Macao. The city is gorgeous. And it was so nice of you to send a limousine to pick me up.

Yes, the plane ride was smooooooth. I'm in the limo now headed toward the hotel. Everything is just amazing. How far is it to the Venetian? Oh, about 20 minutes? Yes, I can... great idea.

I think the readers would appreciate that. I will let them know as soon as I hang up with you.

Thanks for everything M LeMont, I can't wait. We are finally meeting face to face.

The first thing I am going to do is smack you and then I'll give you a big warm bear hug–for making me look at that picture of a fakey woman on your Twitter profile along with some of your crazy, and straight up raw tweets.

The second, for all the golden gems I found after getting past your horse and pony show. You made me work to get to the good stuff."

I pause, surprised at my own sarcasm and also waiting to see how it affects him.

(He said, "Well, I'm not really into the pain thing, so how about a warm kiss on the cheek instead?")

"You gotta deal, I say laughing."

Phew! I was testing the waters there a bit, and it could've been a Tsunami...but we're good. He's such a character, I tell you. "Ok, let me get our readers the post now."

ML wants me to give you guys a Golden Nugget to read while I'm riding to the Hotel. Hold on, let me copy the email and paste it here for everyone to read.

Okay, I just pasted it down below.

Now when you finish reading it, I should be arriving at the hotel where I'll hold the first interview session. Enjoy.

******

Re: M LeMont's Email

Henry Ford said it like this: "If you think you can, and if you think you can't–you are right either way."

Hey, this is M LeMont, and I want to give you something to sink your teeth in while Jennie is on her way to the hotel.

If you're an author, I'm going to make buying this book worth every dime you spent with this one secret.

Old ideas become new and new ideas become old–it's all in the eyes of the beholder. We could be looking at the same thing, but I see it differently, and it gives me an enormous advantage.

Here's what I mean.

I was talking to a client about post-editing her book, and she abhorred the thought of it.

Now I want you to draw close and listen to what I have to say.

Most authors dread self-publishing on Kindle, and when they hit the proverbial publishing button, they never want to see it again until it's time for their next book.

M LeMont: "Well, Lisa it's time to do a little housekeeping and post-edit your book."

Lisa: "What! Post-edit? I'm not supposed to do that. It's been published for over a year now. Who said I even could? I feel bad now. I've done everything I could to publish error-free, and I'm disappointed.

How many errors did you find?"

I said, "No worries, you can fix them."

Lisa: "No, it's too late. I'll just let them be. That's a huge bother, now that it's all been submitted and published."

It was apparent that she was under some notion that you shouldn't fix typos and errors after publishing your book. What was more alarming– her closed mind. She needed to be part of the Think Different Crowd. (TDC), where you exploit and break rules whenever it gives you an upper hand over your opponent. And this was an opportunity because most authors don't post-edit their books for two reasons: psychological and know-how.

Now let me remind you, we live in a digital age, so you don't have to get it right the first time. It's not a print book, so having the ability to make changes after your book is published is paramount.

Shh! Listen to what I'm about to say because it's just one example of why your buying this book will be so valuable for you.

I normally publish two days before the release and buy a copy. Then I read it and fix any errors and republish. I can republish time and again if I want to.

If I have new ideas to improve a scene or write an entirely new one; I can do that.

How many times have you thought of a new line and wished you had written it in your book?

Let me give you an example: One of my followers retweeted an excerpt from my novel Shh! Kiss Me Baby with her comments–

"If I had the time I would give him a taste of what a real woman is and what his money can't buy."

Wow! That was hot and steamy. And six months later after the book was published, I added that line into my book. I'm always making my books better, long after they are published.

Have no fear of post-editing. Embrace the idea and use it to make your books better.

It's part of the Think Different Crowd (TDC) mentality. Be a fearless writer who is not afraid to be unconventional, break traditional norms and practices, leaving the competition standing in the dust.

Four Steps To Post Editing:

- Make changes to the manuscript uploaded to Kindle.
- Upload the revised manuscript to Kindle the same way you did the first time you published it.
- Click the Preview button and view your book on all Kindle devices to make sure edits and changes are correct.

- When you hit the publish button, all changes will override the original book.

During the publishing process your book is still available for purchase. This is good to know.

It takes 12-24 hours for your book changes to appear on Amazon.

Okay guys, I have to meet Jennifer. This is a big moment for us, and I don't want to disappoint her. I just wanted to give you a taste of what's in store for you.

Normally, I would charge $20,000 to meet with a client for a marketing consultation and they would of course pay their own airfare and hotel accommodations.

I've broken my sacred rules here, for reasons I can't fully explain. I've always 'flown solo'– always. I never thought I'd allow myself to be interviewed–or as Jen says, "Have a Collaborative."

And then I think you could just call the rest intuition because she had a unique voice when we communicated about comments related to my book HTG100K or working her Fiverr gigs.

Her casual voice was completely different than her writing style–I saw that beautiful mess of contradictions.

She made me laugh my ass off and had something REAL that came through in her words. I realized her natural gift came through in a conversational writing style.

That's when it hit me–there's a reason for everything and to co-author…..WHAT??

I took a deep breath and put it all on the line–I had to offer her a trip to Macao for an exclusive interview and pick up the tab.

It's obvious that I've been mesmerized by Jen's gift of communication and she's probably the only person that could convince me to reveal my deepest marketing secrets. So let's see what happens.

Chapter 3 Anxious

I can't believe I'm finally here. This place is breath-taking.

Carlos from the jet has been so kind in escorting me toward the entrance of the Resort. I grab his arm gently. I need to let him know I must stop a moment. What looks almost identical to the Piazza San Marco, Basilica in Venice, Italy is directly in front of me.

How can I not take this in? Here I am across the world in Macao, yet staring at a place that I've loved from childhood. The irony, like everything else, it's so thought out, to the minutest of details. The only difference between this view in front of me and Piazza San Marco in Venice, Italy is the lights. They are everywhere. It is magical...feels like I have stepped out onto a movie set.

This place is palatial. We enter and Carlos leads me directly to the glass elevators.

Carlos: Are you alright Señora? You seem a bit nervous.

Jennifer: The truth is, I am nervous because I've been waiting for this moment a long time.

Carlos: Here we are Señora.

I exit the elevator, thanking Carlos. "Muchisimas Gracis por todo." As soon as I say goodbye, someone from the hotel greets me and says, "Jennifer Lopez, right this way. M LeMont is waiting on you."

He escorts me to yet another set of private elevators, leading to the top floor. It seems to take forever. My mind wanders…it was never so much about how M LeMont would look, as just finally meeting the person whose writings I had soaked up for so long. I had already seen LeMont in my mind. His words were my vision of him.

I thank the man who escorted me and walk into the dining area. There are candles on every table and the lighting is low.

I look around, seeing no one dining at any of the tables and there is M LeMont standing near the windows, talking to the Maître d like he owns the place.

He's just as I had envisioned he would be: TALL, DARK, and HANDSOME. He has a gray beard, a shaved head, and a deep mesmerizing voice that would make any woman melt.

He begins walking over to me and getting closer–he says, "You must be Jennifer–let me look into those pretty brown eyes. You are even more beautiful than any words I could use to describe you."

I thought, okay let me clear my head because I can't seem to find the words. I study him quickly with a smile:) I didn't know how this was all going to go, I just knew today was in destiny's hands.

M LeMont reaches out to shake my hand, followed by a big bear hug and a soft kiss on my cheek.

I finally summon the strength to speak. "Hi M LeMont, I'm so glad to meet you. Oh my gosh...at last we meet! This is truly a dream come true and one of the most exciting times of my life.

Oh, and please forgive me if I don't smack you like I said I would for making me come all the way to Macao to uncover the mystery that surrounds you." (Smiling.)

M LeMont: Yea, well that must be one helluva mystery. Plus, I forgot about that smack. (Laughing) Well, I'm sure what you learn will far exceed your time and my money.

Jennifer: I have no doubt. And thank you so much for picking up the tab and sparing no expense. Everything is simply gorgeous.

(*We've always joked that way from the first day. We have never spoken to each other until now, even writing this book has been all by email. It's funny how your personality can shine through your writings. I feel like I already know him.)*

M LeMont: Oh, you don't have to thank me, it's so much my pleasure. Please sit down. I've reserved the entire restaurant and a band to play your favorite music. Now you must be famished from the long trip.

Jennifer: You're amazing. Thank you LeMont.

Chapter 4 The Interview

Jennifer: I'm sitting here with author M LeMont at the fabulous Venetian Macao Resort right off the coast of Hong Kong. I can't believe we're here, kind of surreal, wow! It's that Ineffable feeling–from two people who love words. Now, I have to give you a hug for those precious yellow roses, that was really symbolic ML. (hugging) Oh, it's just beautiful to be here M LeMont. We shouldn't waste any time, let's have our first session.

M LeMont: And you're just as beautiful as the messages we've exchanged on Twitter, nothing happens by chance.

Jennifer: I believe that with all my heart. That's why it became my author's theme for this year: Synchronicity (smiling).

Waiter: 對不起小姐，請問你想喝點什麼？

Excuse me miss, what would you like to drink?

"Oh, I'll have Rum and coke with three limes"

Waiter: 你先生？ "And you sir?"

M LeMont: Lime and Rum is the tipple drink of sailors but with the twist of lime makes it a sassy drink for divas. I'll have the same.

Jennifer: (Smiling) Well, I see this is going to be a wild interview and if anybody follows your tweets they already know you have a way with words. This book–Write Like You're Already Famous will show everyone how to use words to captivate, for effect.

M LeMont: Yes, and by using the right words at the right time, it can make a sentence brilliant and set the tone. I used the words sassy and diva because I don't want anyone to think this is going to be another boring interview. I don't do anything boring.

Jennifer: That is something no one would disagree with.

M LeMont: Well, I'm just gonna lay it out there anyway; just in case you feel offended by the sometimes flirtatious remarks I make with Jennifer–you'd be missing out on a lot of valuable information. We're like peas and carrots JENNAYY and I. (laughing)

Jennifer: Forrest Gump! (big smile) Ok, well, I've already prepped everybody on my end to expect the unexpected. (laughing) Thank God!

M LeMont: I want everyone to know there is some power behind everything that is going to be discussed here. The interview is designed to make you have some light bulb moments as well as change the way you think.

Things are never the way we think they are. So savor every word and listen carefully.

Jennifer: Hey, M LeMont, you may not even know everything that is going to be discussed, so remember who's leading this interview and leave the majority of questions to me. I will make sure we cover as many writing and publishing secrets, as we possibly can. I'm not leaving here without picking your brain. Now, can we talk a bit about collaboration, and why more authors should take advantage of the opportunity to collaborate?

M LeMont: Sure deal. Well, as you know I was dead against collaborations, and if you weren't relentless in your efforts, this interview would never have happened.

Jennifer: Oh, relentless huh? I see how it is now. 'What comes to light,' hajaha! I won't forget how you told me that you 'fly solo' and partnerships don't work.

M LeMont: Yes, but oh, how wrong I was. I see you liked another of my books, 'Caught Up, What's Done In The Dark Comes To Light...' Well, when you find the right person–collaborating can open a floodgate of ideas.

Jennifer: It sure opened up a whole new perspective on writing with us. The flood waters rose so high at one point, I think we almost drown. (laughing again) Ok, seriously now–what do you think is a major problem why most authors shy away from 'Collaboratives'?

M LeMont: The biggest problem with collaborating is that egos, pride and personality clashes can get in the way. People shy away from working together for two reasons:

First, there's a level of selflessness required which can be challenging. Second, collaborating requires individuals to stretch themselves and trust another person enough to share their own individual and valuable insights. This is how precious gems of information are uncovered.

You once called it the Pearl of Great Price, in a post on your– website thejennieration.com. I remember, you said it comes by 'discovering the uniqueness of individual perspectives.' Collaborating can reveal a whole new world of possibilities, whose benefits have far outreaches.

Jennifer: So, you read a little of my writing too, eh? I'm impressed. Pulling the 'Pearl of Great Price' out of your hat. That's so true. There's no ego, no pride, not with our interactions. That's how I knew a "Collaborative" with you would be amazing.

The freedom from ego and pride allow for a "beautiful–mess" that comes with the uniquenesses in our styles and those contradictions–to our similarities.

M LeMont: It's all about creativity–just like the word you used *uniquenesses* there's no such word, but we left it in because we're having a conversation and we're not trying to be politically correct. Plus, it mesmerizes the soul. *Como dulce,* How sweet it is when you find that sweet spot of inspiration.

If anybody wants to know more about collaborations (or as Jen calls them, 'Collaboratives')–we wrote a post on it. It's titled, "Go Ahead, just Wonder" in the second half of the book. If you want to take a few minutes and read it now, you can, but hurry back because this interview is going to begin in five minutes: Golden Nugget #89. Remember this book is designed to change the way you THINK.

******

Jennifer: Well, I think everyone is back with us now. Why do you write in 2nd person POV? I've read three of your books, and you're a brilliant writer. Shh! Kiss Me Baby left me speechless, with three narratives in 1st person POV and 2nd person POV. That takes a lot of nerve.

M LeMont: The only way to stand out from the rest of the crowd is to do something that others are afraid to do. So I studied the works of people who were bold in their approach like author John

Locke, Arnold Schwarzenegger and Quentin Tarantino.

Jennifer: That is an unusual group; an author, actor, and moviemaker? I got John Locke because he writes in 1st & 2nd person, POV, but why Arnold Schwarzenegger and Quentin? I mean, Arnold's not even that great an actor–in my eyes.

M LeMont: Arnold because he talks in short, snappy and powerful phrases like, "I'll Be Back" and "HASTA LA VISTA BABY". If you notice, he never says a lot. But what he says has impact and captivates. I believe short and snappy words, rhythm, and flow keep the readers glued to the story.

And Quentin doesn't do anything conventional–he'll begin a movie at the ending or the middle and go where most screen writers wouldn't dare.

So when writing in 2nd person is done right, you drag the reader into the story as one of the characters. They become a participant instead of a spectator.

Jennifer: That makes perfect sense now. When I read 'Shh! Kiss Me Baby', I didn't just identify with the character Mary Jane, I actually felt I was playing her part. And it was like I felt her emotions. Wow, I can't believe I told you that? (Blushing)

M LeMont: It's okay honey, I understand, my writings have that that kind of affect on people. I'm just joking–see I got you smiling already. Anyway, you want readers to feel what you're saying whether it's fiction, non-fiction, or a how-to book. So I do a lot of little things to keep my audience engaged.

Jennifer: You're really crazy, you know that ML? (smiling) But here's what really shocked me. You stopped in the middle of a scene and began talking directly to the reader, and asking them questions about Mary Jane. Wow, you just pulled me right in.

M LeMont: (laughing heartily) I know, one of my readers said he caught himself answering me when he was reading How To Gain 100,000 Twitter Followers. It's all part of the new wave of thinking and doing things nobody else would dare do. It gives your reader a fresh reading experience.

Jennifer: Wait a minute, let me get this straight: You wrote HTG100K, a How-to book in 2nd person, and then you wrote this book around a narrative story? How dare you? I'm just joking because I read HTG100K and it was the most entertaining and informative How-To book I've ever read. 90+ Positive reviews–that's proof enough. And the verdict is still out on this book.

M LeMont: Yea, I guess you can say the jury is still out on this book–but we don't worry about specific results, now do we? We write it with the attitude that anything goes. And that's why it's different because we push the boundaries to make it different.

Jennifer: Most authors write in 3rd person POV– aren't you taking a risk of offending your audience if you talk directly to them?

M Le'Mont: Yes, you do run a risk, but the rewards are tremendous if you can pull it off. The reason most authors write in 3rd POV is because it's safe. And that's the way they were taught in school. It's a crutch that leads to long and boring narrations, description and setup.

Plus, it presents the author as if he's omniscient, knowing what each character is thinking and this leads him into TELLING the story instead of pulling back the curtains and SHOWING what's happening with more action and dialogue.

Jennifer: So the three elements to focus on in order to write a great book that stands out from the crowd are: Style, Rhythm, and Flow?

M LeMont: Yes, and I would add a fourth, 'Beats.' I know it sort of sounds like writing a song, but beats are short and snappy nouns and verbs that make a sentence like sweet music to your readers' ears.

Jennifer: That's a perfect description. Is there another author's writing style you like?

M LeMont: I study the works of Shonda Rhimes.

Jennifer: Oh my gosh LeMont, I'm reading her book Year of Yes. She's the creator of Grey's Anatomy, Scandal, and How To get Away with Murder.

M LeMont: That's right, Shonda owns Thursday Night on ABC. She's the epitome of what this book is all about: Freedom to be you, mixed with a little bit of fear. Shonda is a great storyteller–writes in first & second person. She even stops in the middle of a sentence and talks directly to her readers–like we do here.

In her own words here's how she described her writing from a speech she wrote for Dartmouth College:

"PITHY. WITTY. SNAPPY."

Jennifer: Hmm... That's sounds a lot like the way you write and what you've been telling us.

M LeMont: Exactly. Maybe one day her Client and my Client can get together. Then Shonda and I can Co-author a book. (Laughing.) I would love it.

Jennifer: I'm sure you would like that, ML. Our readers would have to get her book to find out her definition of Client. She does say some shocking things that make you say, Wow! I can't believe she said that.

M LeMont: Shonda became famous by writing like she was already famous and one day a network like ABC took notice. She's over the top funny, witty and shocking. So get her book–watch her shows and study them.

Jennifer: That's good advice. Don't Write To Be Famous, Write Like You're Already Famous.

******

Jennifer: Give us the Hashtag secrets? I see that you use as many as 7 when everyone else is using 2 Hashtags.

M LeMont: Yes, Hashtags are the BIG little secret.

—Shh! Draw Close, Listen—

Just in case, someone doesn't know what the hell Hashtags are, here's a brief explanation. Hashtags allow you to categorize information so people can find it. If you are selling a product, then you would add a tag to your tweet or headline.

When you add the # before a word like #SocialMedia then anyone looking for topics on Social Media will click on the link.

Now here's the BIG little Secret.

Hashtags give you the ability to reach an entirely different market outside of the people who follow you. Think of each Hashtag as a market unto itself. People follow Hashtags like they follow people on Twitter.

Jennifer: What? Hashtags have their own followers?

M LeMont: Yes, that is correct. In reality, you don't need any followers if you know the magic of Hashtags. But, if you did have a lot of followers it would expand your reach even farther.

Jennifer: This is intriguing. Why don't you give me some examples of a headline with Hashtags that you wrote...

M LeMont: Here's a tweet I wrote with plenty of Hashtags: **Make Your Tweets Stand Out.** getBook.at/HTG100K #Twitter #Authors #Writers #SMM #Ian1 #SocialMedia #SmallBitz #Marketing

Jennifer: Oh, I see, it literally opens up a whole segment of individuals who are specifically interested in these topics. Look, there's even great ideas for small start up businesses out of the home if you're a writer who needs extra income. It's all right here when I key in the Hashtag #SmallBiz on Twitter. That's pretty cool. What does #Ian1 mean? It doesn't seem clear when I type it in because there's a lot of random tweets in here. So, what made you select that Hashtag? Also, How can I find out which are the most popular Hashtags?

M LeMont: The Hashtag Ian1 is Independent Authors Network, it's an organization that helps self-published authors. The Hashtag ranking is 69% so it's widely used.

Jennifer: Okay and now, can I find out, which are the most popular Hashtags?

M LeMont: Well, there is a special app I use that rates the popularity of Hashtags. Naturally you don't want to use a Hashtag that has zero popularity because nobody's following those. Go to: Hashtagify.me and type any Hashtag. You want to use the Hashtags with highest ratings: 50 and higher.

I've written a Golden Nugget, #6 to give you more information.

Jennifer: That is a critical piece of marketing information ML, and I see why you use as many Hashtags as Twitter's 140 characters will allow.

M LeMont: The so-called experts will tell you not to use any more than 2 Hashtags because it looks ugly. Well, in the world of pretty–ugly stands out. I love going against popular beliefs, and that's what this book is designed to do–make you think differently. And it makes you say–why not? Why, can't I do it this way?

Jennifer: I love it. You definitely swim upstream and against the current of 'the follower fish.' That's why I like to think of you as the flying fish… the one who flies AND swims. You get it done, no matter how you need to get there. Wow, I've learned so much already. I will make sure to read the Golden Nugget #6. I also noticed that you use a custom made link for all your books. Is there any significance besides that it looks cool?

getBook.at/ShhKissMeBaby
getBook.at/HTG100K

M LeMont: You have a keen eye, don't you? Jennaayyy? The answer is yes–there is a HUGE benefit, more than what you see on the surface.

Jennifer: Well, as you have said, if you're going to be a good writer/marketer then you must study the best. And I've read all your Golden Nuggets–plus, I pay attention to even the littlest of details.

M LeMont: The custom book link is more than just pretty–looks. First, it's subliminal and tells your prospects what to do–like an immediate call to action after striking an individual emotion.

(i.e. getBook.at/HTG100K)

Now Open Your Eyes Wide and Pay Attention This Is A Critical Point.

I'm going to tell you what's been killing off your book sales. When a prospect from another country clicks on your book link to buy it or get more information–they are taken to Amazon's sales page in the country that you live in and when they click the buy button, the order is declined with a prompt that says: *Sorry, you are unable to purchase in this country.*

Jennifer: What, they aren't directed to the right country? So the prospect thinks the book isn't available in their country?

M LeMont: That is correct they think the book isn't available in their country. Amazon has about 13 different country codes and where you reside falls within one of those different codes. Someone sent me a direct message that said he was unable to buy my book because it wasn't available in Romania. Now that's rare that you would even hear from a prospect. So I sent him the correct link for AmazonRomania.com. Later, he sent a message, "Thank you, I just downloaded your book."

Jennifer: First of all, it's awesome that someone reached out to you like that–shows they understood the value of your book. Okay, I'm dying to hear the solution? I know we can't list 13 country codes on every blog post and send 13 URLS with every tweet.

M LeMont: The solution is to use a universal book link. I use Booklinker.net an app that converts your Amazon page to the country code your prospect lives in. It's simple to use– just insert your book link and then select your custom link and you're done.

Jennifer: Great! So, many authors and readers are going to be grateful for this information ML. Are there more of these invisible forces that prevent authors from making sales?

M LeMont: Yes, there are several more, and you can read about them and the solutions in the Golden Nugget section of this book–it's priceless information, Jen.

Jennifer: You realize you are a rare golden nugget yourself, don't you? I mean think about it. How many people would share ALL of this valuable information for others in what amounts to the Best Resource Book out there on the topics of Writing, Marketing, Social Media & every "HOW TO" imaginable for such a fair price? This is crazy–you are crazy ML–you aught to be charging people more because the benefits are there, no denying it. I mean, people can do so much to help themselves and you make it so darn easy.

M LeMont: I want people to learn. I always have. My writing is a passion. I do it every day. I have years of experience in the business world and the people who go through my site know. This is my way of sharing it all in one place. I don't care about the money and that's a fact. I want to get the information out there and I want to help people.

Jennifer: Just one more reason I knew you'd be the best Collaborative I ever had. You represent everything they stand for to me: sharing from an authentic place and doing it without "getting your shadow in the way." You and I really are like peas and carrots. I think I am going to have to retire after this interview because you blew it out the water.

M LeMont: Now, that's a good idea. Maybe we can retire together to some faroff island some place and write forever or until we can't stand it anymore!

Jennifer: Uh... I think we better switch gears on that one. (Laughing) Okay, so the other day you told me to run my Twitter like a talk radio show. I've never heard anything like that before. Can you expound?

M LeMont: What I meant by that is, Twitter gives you a microphone to be whatever you want to be. And it's up to you to decide what that is. The internet is the #1 social activity for most people, and they go there to be entertained. So in my mind, I'm the host of a talk radio show when I get on Twitter.

Jennifer: Yes, you are–and sometimes–a very controversial host. But you make it fun, and you interact a lot with your audience. The talk radio thing, is that all in your mind (smiling) or is that what your followers call it too?

M LeMont: Well, I don't know what they call it, they could call it turtle soup or something. (Laughing) But it's what I call it that matters.

It's all about changing your thinking about how you look at things.

I treat Twitter the same way Rush Limbaugh and Howard Stern treat their talk radio shows. They show up for an hour or two prepared to have fun, entertain, and inform.

Jennifer: I love it. You kill me, you just do. Ok, I am grabbing a post you tweet when you come on Twitter. It's has a dark background and white border. Here it is.

Who Is M LeMont?

Modest... Brilliant! Genius! Magnificent!

That's what they called me when I wrote How To Gain 100,000 Twitter Followers, but it's not true. I just showed up and went to work. Showing up is 90% of the battle, and you'll look to others like you've climbed Mt Everest.

Understanding...

This year, give everyone a nice book to read. What! Another FREAKIN book?

Wait a minute...IT AIN'T MY FAULT you gave them the WRONG book.

Helpful...

I'd give everybody a dollar if they used this one secret that would help so Damn much.

Advisor to many...

If you want to succeed, learn all you can, and then break the rules. And, that Masters Degree? Throw the damn thing in the dump, it'll make you think you're entitled to something.

Honest....

I'm not for everyone and neither are you. Stop making stupid people famous.

Trusting...

I like Donald T. But he's a liar. I don't believe anybody that says trust me. It's the cry out of the guilty.

Jennifer: That is the best. It's YOU and it's one of the things that got me right away when I was on your actual page. And, although I wouldn't throw my degrees in the dump, I agree with everything else. Some of the most educated people I know are completely self-taught. I never thought about turning my Twitter account into a talk radio show? But I am now.

M LeMont: Your Twitter account is prime real estate in the sky. What are you going to do to make it valuable and attract tourists like Disneyworld? People want to be entertained, and have fun, and be informed.

Jim Rohn said, "Find a way to serve the many, for service to the many leads to greatness."

Jennifer: Great quote. Where do you find your content?

M LeMont: I'm very selective with what I tweet and what goes in my time-line. I curate most of my stuff right on Twitter. I very seldom go outside of my main stream. I look for Gifs, graphics, videos, and pictures that I can retweet and make funny comments on. I also look for valuable and useful content. If you like, you can click here and check out my time-line. @mistersalesman

Jennifer: You know what M LeMont? I am lovin' this chat. Ok, I am on your timeline and I see the way you're interacting here with the readers. So you just grab stuff that you think your followers are interested in?

M LeMont: That's right, and the only way you know your audience is to test them with different things and see how many unfollowers you get the next day. Then you know not to retweet that type of content again.

Jennifer: So the idea behind the talk radio concept is don't wait to be famous to do these things, but do them now and Be that person.

M LeMont: ¡Correcto Perfecto!–It's a mindset or attitude that can be applied to any thing. It makes you see and think differently than everyone else. And running your Twitter account like a talk radio show is a good example of how to act like you're Already Famous.

Jennifer: Do you interview people on your Twitter talk radio show?

M LeMont: Yes, I do, but they are impromptu interviews, they don't know it's an interview live on Twitter. At the end of the conversation, I ask if they've ever watched Candid Camera. Then bust it out–'Well, you are on AHA Live with M LeMont and this was a live interview.'

Jennifer: Wow! I bet they nearly pass out. Don't EVER do that with me please, and I mean it! I'm NOT the lover of surprises–at all and I would never forgive you for it!

M LeMont: Okay, relax honey! I know! You like to be in control! (on top–laughing) Yea, they are quite surprised. I then take the notes and compile them into an interview and post them on my website. It's good exposure for an author.

Jennifer: Hey, that was some powerful stuff you laid on us. Let's take a potty break and if you can give the readers the link to one of the interviews they can read it during the break.

M LeMont: Great idea–that's why we are co-authors–we are always in sync. Here's the link to the impromptu interview I did with Rochelle Campbell. (PC users hold down the control button.)
http://mistersalesman.com/AHA_Rochelle_Campbell.php

Jennifer: I do love the sound of that: co-author with M LeMont. Ok, we will be back in 2 min 2 seconds...

******

Jennifer: Okay, we're back with more questions for M LeMont.

Waiter: I'm sorry to interrupt, 我很抱歉打斷，你會像沙漠？我們有各種美味的項目可供選擇。would you like desert? We have a variety of delicious items to choose from.

Jennifer: Oooh, what is this, chocolate cake?

Waiter:
那麼，它就像一個蛋糕，但它不是蛋糕。這是一個土生葡人的食譜。你想嚐嚐嗎？ Well, it's like a cake, but it's not cake. It's a very old Macanese recipe. Would you like to taste?

Jennifer: Hmm... That's delicious with the ice cream and raspberry sauce on top. I'll have some of that, thank you. What's your name?

Waiter: My name is JIANG, it means a great river, Yang-tzŭ.

Jennifer: Well, JIANG, that's a nice name and you speak English very well. Can you tell me about that beautiful statue by the waterfall in the lobby?

Waiter: 它是由当地艺术家的名字陈超 It's called EROS and was made by a famous sculptor, named Chao Chen, who studied Greek mythology. The hotel purchased it from his personal collection. Years ago, the artist met a beautiful woman at a waterfall. They never saw or spoke to one another again for 10 years. He believed that destiny would eventually bring them back together. So throughout those ten years he worked on this statue of Eros, who you see there presenting a crown made of an olive branch to this goddess. The inscription at the bottom reads, "My soul knew before I did." 我的靈魂就知道在我之前

Jennifer: What a touching story. Art always carries with it, a story. The story makes the art that much more beautiful. So, did he ever get to present this his labor of love to her?

Waiter: 而對於你，先生？ You know, I actually have never been asked. I need to find out the answer to this question and get back to you. It is most certainly worth finding out.

M LeMont: That's a wonderful story and a magnificent piece of art. Thank you for sharing it with us. I'll also take a piece of that chocolate cake for dessert.

******

Jennifer: Let's get into the thick of it and talk about marketing. That dreaded subject no author wants to talk about. Experts say write more books and the marketing will take care of itself. Is that what we should do?

M LeMont: I look at books as products and the more products, the more money you'll make. But at some point, you have to stop making products and start making sales or you'll go out of business. That's just plain common sense. So whatever expert said to keep writing and the marketing will take care of itself is full of shit.

Jennifer: Well, that's putting it bluntly. (laughing) Please, tell us more.

M LeMont: Here's the secret formula: Marketing is 99% and Product 1%. If people don't know that your book exists, then it doesn't matter how good it is. Even bad books out-sell because of excellent marketing. And they keep selling even with bad reviews as long as the marketing is outstanding.

Jennifer: Yes, I know I've gotten some New York Times Bestsellers and they were so terrible I couldn't finish reading them. But I never bought a steamy book like your, Shh! Kiss Me Baby–and that was just to see if this "business guy" could pull off what he was marketing so HARD. (both laugh) But I did hear from a freaky single girlfriend of mine that 50 Shades of Grey had dismal sales for 3 years and bad reviews. Being 'freaky,' she of course bought it anyway, but would have been much happier with your book. What a waste of money in my opinion, that '50 Shades of Stupidity!'–Critics even said it was poorly written. We could've written a better one with some spice–right. (laughing) But I also heard once the trailer was released–ropes and chains hit an all time high. The marketers must have struck some emotional chords. Your book, Shh! Kiss Me Baby actually should be turned into a movie. Women everywhere would search the world over for Buddy Brown. But don't you worry ML, if they can't find someone to play Mary Jane, I'll take the part for a nominal fee.

M LeMont: Oh honey, you would be the perfect Mary Jane, so the rest of 'em would have to just wait in line for the flick. (I guess at one point that 50 Shades book was selling at a rate of one book per second. It's all about marketing–and if you get the marketing right then you can sell any product whether it's good or bad, whether the product works or not. Don't believe me? Then take a look at all the weight loss products on the Internet. Even in spite of bad product reviews, people are still buying because of good marketing that evokes emotions.

Jennifer: The world is so backwards, upside down and inside out sometimes. That's why I love that we can always talk about the mess of contradictions and we just "get each other."

Okay what about the experts that say it's a waste of time to build a social media platform on Twitter?

M LeMont: The first problem is they don't know how to build a Twitter Platform and second, they think Twitter is a platform to sell products. That's why you see a lot spamming with constant tweets like 'BUY MY BOOK.'

But Twitter is a platform to LAUNCH products, not sell them. There's a big difference.

Desire+Unique Moment in Time=Action

Jennifer: That's true marketing. The best part–*when you are selling something truly worthy of the customer's purchase–the marketing creates an authentic connection–people FEEL.*

Hmm, I'm thinking that's how I was drawn to you. Your posts and 'story' intersected with a unique moment in time for sure–and I knew I wanted to learn more. I remember retweeting a great post of yours recently and a follower commenting, "Okay, I'm buying your HTG100K book now."

I wondered how many of your posts she read to get to the point that it was time to buy.

M LeMont: She read some great interactive tweets and got involved in the conversation…that helped build her interest. Also, on average a prospect needs to read 5 of your posts to have confidence in you and your product. That's why you should write a post every day with a specific emotion you are trying to spark in your readers.

Jennifer: Writing a post every day will definitely help improve your craft as a writer, and separate you from the crowd. I look forward to reading your posts every day and usually go straight to your page to find them. I do that with the few people I really admire in my feed. I go straight to their page instead of scrolling the newsfeed.

M LeMont: And it doesn't matter whether it's a post or an email marketing list you should write every day to hone your writing skills and to find your loyal fans who will become your customers.

Jennifer: Okay speaking about fans, here's something a little different. I have a question here from one of our readers. "Why are my loyal fans and followers not buying my books, even after they click on my book link? I've tried everything and nothing works. So what I'm I doing wrong??"

M LeMont: Well, there are a lot of things going on behind the scenes that interfere with the buying process. There's an estimated 80% of users who access the Internet using a mobile device, cell, tablet and not a PC.

Jennifer: Wow, 80%! I know I use my tablet or cell to access the Internet, every day. Now, that should be good news for authors–easy internet access means more people on-line, more link clicks and book sales, right?

M LeMont: You would think, but most of those people don't have a Kindle and what makes matters worse is they don't know about the Kindle free app for Cell, Tablet, and PC.

Jennifer: That's crazy. So people can download the actual Kindle app...no need to specifically own a separate Kindle. Pretty great–and it's listed on the Amazon site…hmm you'd think people would just know to click on the app there in Amazon.

M LeMont: Well, these prospects may be first time e-book buyers or people who typically buy print books. Either way, the "Download Free App" link is so small that you wouldn't necessarily see it unless you were looking for it.

Jennifer: Okay, that makes sense. So what's the solution though for all these loyal followers who just aren't buying author's books–because I know you have one? (smiling)

M LeMont: We must make people aware of the free Kindle app. So I tweet a message about it every day. I also display it on every post on my website, and when I give someone my book link, I also give them a link to the free Kindle app to download.

Here's the message:

If you don't have a Kindle, download the free app for cell, pc or tablet http://amzn.to/1BtVqdO

Jennifer: Well, it sure worked for me because I was one of those people. I stop every week at a little local resale bookshop and definitely love traditional books. It wasn't until I met you that I even considered reading a book electronically, even though I have plenty of friends who find that is the only way they want to read. I never thought I'd be one of those people, but since I wanted to read your book badly enough–I did everything you suggested and just as you described it here. Yours were the first official e-books I'd ever read. And I love it now, because it's right there in my cell phone so I go back and refer to things whenever I like, especially parts I highlighted. I love that feature.

Another really neat thing you do–which not all authors do…you give the reader a chance to share your book 1x for 14 days. When I saw that for the first time, I couldn't believe it. There's so many advantages to it. Have you gotten a lot of great feedback?

M LeMont: Of course, Twitter is a great place to test ideas. I've had many people thank me for making them aware of the free Kindle app, and others thank me after they bought my books. It's hard to convince authors that they are losing sales, and that is why Loyal fans and followers are not buying their books.

Jennifer: Now they will definitely know. Do we have a Golden Nugget Post to share with the readers now while we (devour each other–I mean) this indescribably yummy Chocolate Cake?

M LeMont: (Laughing) Yes, Golden Nugget Post #2.

Jennifer: Wow, this is just a lot of valuable information you're dispensing here. I really appreciate it. Two things that frustrate most people on Twitter are the automated tweets and direct messages.

It seems super impersonal and takes away from the authentic interaction with people–ya' know–being sociable. What do you think about automation?

M LeMont: If you can't beat 'em then join 'em. Automate Everything! Let me explain before somebody has a heart attack. When you automate it will actually give you MORE time to interact with people and write and market your books. But where people go wrong is they automate and then leave, go off to the beach, sip a few Margaritas and disappear from Twitter totally. We're looking for an advantage and disappearing is not it.

Jennifer: You got that right. It's like Groundhog Day when you go to the page of someone who has the same strands running all day and you know 'no one's home.' Such a better idea…to automate but then use the time that has freed up to interact with more people and then you really have the perfect combination of tweets, retweets and book promotions. Nobody would even know you're automated.

M LeMont: That really is the key, that perfect combination, and it creates a great blending of all the elements. If you think of yourself as a radio talk show host, then it becomes fun, entertaining and informative. You don't have to be concerned about agitating people with the automation, you still promote your books to pay the bills but it's more in the form of a commercial break.

Jennifer: Are there any scheduler companies that you recommend?

M LeMont: I use TweetJukeBox.com, Hootsuite.com and Buffer.com. I also feel the same way about Direct messages. As a matter of fact, I was so disgusted at one point and had reached my limit, that I even wrote a blog begging people to stop sending direct messages for sales solicitations. And then I thought it over and decided again, if I can't beat them why not join them and show them how. (laughing)

Jennifer: That's the M LeMont I know.

M LeMont: You see, most solicitors are amateurs and don't know the first thing about marketing. So I decided to automate one direct message thanking people for the follow and add a little message about my book and link. The feedback and sales have actually been outstanding. So I suggest everyone to give it a try and monitor it carefully. One automated DM message, just one time seems to work.

Jennifer: That's another interesting one. Especially with all the negative hype over sending auto DM's. Do you have an example of the auto DM message?

M LeMont: I certainly do:

Thank you for the follow. If you have any questions about Twitter ask me. I'm not only the Author of a Bestseller Twitter book, How To Gain 100,000 Twitter Followers–I'm also a CLIENT. I USE the strategies every day to gain over 200,000 followers.

http://getBook.at/HTG100K Twitter secrets revealed.

If you don't have a kindle download the free app for cell, pc or tablet http://amzn.to/1BtVqdO

Jennifer: So, one time is a good thing–to let people know you appreciate the follow and tell them what you are about. Ok. I appreciate that. M LeMont, a true writer AND marketer. You most certainly are… among other things, I will add. (laughing)

M LeMont: There you go again honey, always razzin' me! Hey Jennayy–you're a big fan of my novel, Shh! Kiss Me Baby, right?

Jennifer: You know I am. And for someone who doesn't make time to read steamy novels–I was initially only reading it to see what your writing style would be like for such a different genre, especially after reading your How to Gain 100K on Twitter. I thought, "Can this guy pull off a Romance when he writes about business?" But you wow'd me once again: a story within a story, multiple narratives…and well–ya know–I don't want to get a hot-flash talkin' about it.

M LeMont: Oh, I know honey, it moved you like sugar to your soul, right? Ok, well I was leaving this as a surprise for the end of our interview–I know how much you LOVE surprises. (joking) But I just had to…guess who's here in Macao?

Jennifer: Oh geez, are you really going to throw a surprise in here now? The surprises are my job–remember…? …revealing the secrets of M LeMont to the Twitter world. I should have guessed you'd throw a curve ball! So What is it?? (anxious)

M LeMont: Ok, well look behind you.

Jennifer: (turning around anxiously, she sees a man walking up and thinks–oh my gosh, is this? He looks like a famous actor...)

M LeMont: I want you to meet the real Buddy Brown, lead character and narrator of the book, Shh! Kiss Me Baby Heyyyy Buddy! I knew you wouldn't miss a chance to come and meet my one and only, Jennifer C. Lopez.

Buddy Brown: (Reaching out to give Jennifer a handshake and hug.)

Jennifer: This is too much for any one woman to handle–so great but totally and completely unexpected! Buddy, I've got to give you a big kiss on the cheek and I hope that's gonna be ok with you, I mean now that your days as a lady's man are all meant for one special Mary Jane and your daughter Jasmine.

Buddy Brown: You bet it is Jennifer. My absolute pleasure.

Jennifer: Your character became a part of my heart and now, you are not just a character anymore…well maybe you'll always be a 'character"– huh?? (laughter)

This sort of thing just doesn't happen. I am so thrilled to know you, especially since you are the most precious friend to M LeMont. Buddy, I must ask–how does it feel to be back in Macao? Must be some of the most beautiful, passionate memories…sure are for me, and I was only there in fiction. (smiling)

Buddy Brown: Well, it most definitely brings back memories, no doubt–you know. "Life has a way of testing your sincerity…" as you know from reading our story. That was my time to wake up about a lot of things.

Jennifer: I can imagine. Those were some intense and even sacred moments you spent here with Mary Jane. So, did you ride in from the airport in a Red Lamborghini or was it a sexy black Limo with a feisty female driver?

Buddy Brown: Ah you remember, ha-ha. Well, you know things have changed quite a bit since the last time I was in Macao.

Jennifer: It sure was one hell of a ride, though wasn't it–the story?

Buddy Brown: You know it Jen. And this tall guy standing next to us, well he'd have to be the best friend a guy could ask for. M told me about the interview and that you were someone who really "got him," so I wanted to surprise.

Jennifer: You melt my heart, both of you. Is it okay if I ask you a question about the book Buddy? You and M LeMont both narrated it with quite a bit of surprise and I've never seen it done quite that way before. I'm an avid book reader.

I HAVE to know how you came up with the idea of calling Lena on the phone to talk to the readers while you were at the rodeo with Mary Jane? That must have been incredibly complicated to write and deliver.

Buddy Brown: It certainly was and everyone told us we couldn't do something like that–to stop in the middle of the scene and say, "you know I could tell you what happened that night, but I would mess it up, so let me call Lena on the phone and let her tell you herself." The craziest thing about that is Lena thought she was only telling the story to me, not the whole world.

Jennifer: Wow, I know. I can't even think about that scene without blushing. That is beyond steamy! What an unusual character Lena is–and Fioni too–crazy spicy free spirits in the story. Mary Jane must really be something special to get you to change your playboy ways Buddy.

Then, when you are telling the story to Screen Writer, Daniel Beard III and ask M LeMont to take the story from there because it was too painful for you to relive. What a scene. I connected with the feeling of appreciation for that kind of loyalty.

Buddy Brown: And that is what this book you and M LeMont are writing is all about, taking chances and doing things nobody else dares.

Jennifer: "Live like you were dying"...Tim McGraw.

M LeMont: Ha! The song that brought it all together for Buddy and Mary Jane.

Buddy Brown: Awww, Jen you remind me a lot of Mary Jane. I think you two would be amazingly good friends, in fact I know it. And, you both each have the one daughter, funny.

Jennifer: I know Buddy, I think we would be. I relate to her and I know other readers do too. Loved her lack of pretentiousness, her appreciation of the simple things and yet her contradictions–the intensely passionate side and her daring nature with a willingness to reach outside of her comfort zone.

I wish she was here with you, but this has been more of a surprise than I could have ever asked for.

M LeMont: Should we tell her now Buddy?

Jennifer: Tell me what? (curious)

Buddy Brown: Let's just leave it at this: One day you will meet both Mary Jane and Jasmine. That's all I'm going to say.

M LeMont: Yes, good idea Buddy, such an illusionist.

Jennifer: Ahemmm…look who's talkin' ML!

Well, I want to get across to our readers that anything goes when you write without constraints or conformity... Anything.

Buddy Brown: Yep, exactly how we wrote Shh! Kiss Me Baby–without any fear of criticism, rejection or how it all would exactly turn out. We viewed the whole process like we were creating instead of writing a book. That way it kept us coming up with exciting twists and turns in the book. And actually we had 3 narrators if you included Mary Jane.

Jennifer: Well, I know THIS book with all the Golden Nuggets will be one that readers will pick up time and time again. My honor and privilege for these moments– "Ineffable!"

Buddy Brown: Alright my friends, I've gotta head up to my room and settle in for a bit. (looks over to M...)

M LeMont: (smiling...go ahead tell her.)

Buddy Brown: Jennifer, we know how you don't like surprises so I'll make this quick: Here are two tickets to the Adele Concert World Tour in Paris.

Jennifer: You're kidding me, right!??! I don't even know what to say to the both of you. Adele is one of my absolute favorite artists. How did you know? These tickets are so... (Heart pounding–voice shaking and then …passes out.)

M LeMont: (Jennifer, collapses in my arms.)

******

Paramedics were quick on scene–Jennifer was hyperventilating from all the excitement and exhaustion from the flight.

Twenty four hours later... at breakfast.

Jennifer: Oh my gosh LeMont, I'm so embarrassed! I guess I couldn't handle the excitement last night, after such a long flight...the only thing I remember was the Adele concert. Oh, I don't even know right now. Thank you so much. Hey, I still have a few questions I want to ask if that's okay?

M LeMont: Sure, are you feeling up to it or do you want to go and take a tour of Macao and the beautiful mountainside?

Jennifer: Yes, I would absolutely love to, but I have a question about self-publishing that I may forget to ask in all this excitement unless I do it now. Is that okay with you?

M LeMont: Of course, go right ahead.

Jennifer: There are so many things you have to pay attention to as a self-published author. We all know how important it is to have a well-designed book cover and that perfect title. Is there anything else authors should pay attention to when a prospect lands on their Amazon book page?

M LeMont: The book cover and title are the first things that catch a prospects attention. It's like when a pretty woman walks into the party and all eyes focus on her. Men, women, and haters all take a look. Seen anyone like that?

Jennifer: Of course, I know what you mean. She's the type that commands attention.

M LeMont: Right, but when you sit down and talk with her you find out that she wasn't what you thought–conversation was dull, flat, and shallow–nothing that made a man want her except for a pretty face. The same is true with your book Description–it's what sells the book after a prospect sees the pretty cover and title. You got it?

Jennifer: I definitely do. It goes back to the whole authenticity thing. The cover HAS to reflect what is inside because in THIS case–contradictions wouldn't be good. You sure know how to paint a picture. That's what we should be doing is creating desire in the cover and the description.

M LeMont: The problem for most authors is they write a dull and boring description because they are writing as an author and not as a marketer.

What you have to do is take your author's hat off and THINK like a marketer. Write the description to create desire & evoke emotions to either hit the buy button or take a Look Inside the book.

Jennifer: So there's a buying process that the prospect goes through and you must know it.

M LeMont: 'The Look Inside' feature is also part of the buying process. It's your final opportunity to get the sale. So in your description you want to direct the prospect to either Buy Now or Look Inside your book and read 10% Free.

Jennifer: One thing I want to say here ML. This was something that really stood out to me when I did the "Look Inside" on your "How To Gain 100K Twitter Followers."

I knew it was more than it's title, but what impressed me above all, was you allowing the readers to see such a nice chunk of your book. That seriously impressed me and I thought, this guy is showing the real deal and I can see he knows what he's talking about.

M LeMont: Good honey! You would be surprised how many prospects are unaware of that feature. Now that would also mean you want to put your best content in the first 10% of your book.

Jennifer: Well, not sure how you really say that when the whole book was full of awesome content. I learned until the end and refer back to it as well. But I get that the opening scene has to rock. No long boring narrations and set up. Open with canons blasting, hard-hitting action and dialogue. This is your shot at getting the sale.

M LeMont: That's right, you gotta "get em where you want them" and that's inside your book.

I might also mention that Amazon Search Engines use the Description page to scan for keywords that browsers are searching for. So make sure to include keywords in your description, those you think browsers would use.

Jennifer: I know you're always experimenting and discovering new things–do you plan on offering updates to this book?

M LeMont: Yes, I do plan on offering updates. It's an excellent way to add value and notify our readers when things change.

Jennifer: How will authors get updates--will you send a PDF via email?

M LeMont: I will send an email letting you know where the update is located in the book. But first, you must turn on the automatic update feature on Amazon.

Jennifer: What on Amazon? You mean, the book is not automatically updated.

M LeMont: No, I guess that's another secret I need to tell everyone about, uh?

Jennifer: Yes, because I didn't know about the "Update" feature and I'm sure some of our readers don't know neither.

M LeMont: Okay, go to your account on Amazon.com and at the top far right of the screen, Click on your account. Then click Manage Content and Devices. Scroll down and turn on Automatic Book Updates. Done!

Jennifer: That is a great feature. So how can our readers sign up to be notified for updates?

M LeMont: Just send me an email: bob@mistersalesman.com or go to MLeMont and click on Contact. http://mlemont.com

Jennifer: AWESOME. I've learned so much. Thank you for collaborating with me.

M LeMont: Miel (honey) the feeling is mutual. It has been a fun project. Flying solo to collaborating sure has changed my world. I will never be the same. Jen, you represent authenticity and goodness in your desire to bring people together.

It's everything your "Collaborative" website (thejennieration.com) stands for and I see clearly, why you encourage everyone to work together on projects–you do it with such eloquence and grace.

Plus, your efforts allowed me to share my knowledge in a unique way and hopefully encourage our readers to use these *Critically Valuable Tools* in their writing and marketing. Gracias to you from my heart, writing partner.

Jennifer: Awe that's so sweet...I just knew we could do something special. You always go the extra mile to share valuable information and you've never shy'd away from an OPPORTUNITY to Think Differently and "call it like you see it."

Now you've put so much into this interview I know you're probably exhausted.

M LeMont: I want to go and enjoy the city with you. You know me, I am not a sleeper. I work and write and work some more. I like it that way. (smiles all around)

Jennifer: That sounds great. I would love to see the sights and then relax a bit by reading your Golden Nuggets on my long flight back home.

******

I knew the kind of certainty, the conviction I had that drew me to learn more about M LeMont was something that would only come around once in my lifetime and I was humbled by the whole experience.

I never got around to asking M the questions about the mystery that surrounds him. It was something I had waited for a long time. I guess I am realizing that it really shouldn’t matter, but I am not the type to give up so easily. I have to let it go *for now* and trust that all things come to light in the right time.

What mattered most was meeting him and the powerful things he was willing to share... amazing.

And I will never forget what he said, "Our friendship transcends all boundaries and time and we are bonded forever."

Please enjoy the rest of the book. I know I will.

A Note from M LeMont
Golden Nuggets

"Knowledge is power when it's turned into Action otherwise, it's just someone's head full of wasted information."

Now that was some powerful stuff that you just read. I want to thank you for making it this far.

Unfortunately for some of you, your journey will end here, not because I say so, but because the next part of the book is more intense and not for everybody.

I've reserved it for those who seriously want to learn a unique approach to writing and marketing and who are willing to devour every word until it's soaked into their subconscious mind.

There are over 100 Golden Nuggets packed with powerful information for you to study and analyze.

These essays are called Golden Nuggets for Good Reason. They are actual marketing pieces to distribute valuable, relevant and consistent content that ultimately, lead to increased sales. Many of them have a call to action at the end that relates to a link of one of my books, so don't get bent out of shape.

It's the best way to show what real marketing is all about and get you in the habit of including product links to your posts and email lists, etc.

The Nuggets will open a whole new world of Content Marketing Sorcery.

Each Nugget will take approximately 2 minutes 2 seconds to read–don't try to read all of them at once. Read three or four at a time–study them over a few days and implement the ideas, then come back and read some more.

I guarantee that you won't like all of them, but nevertheless, there are valuable lessons in each one if you slow down and concentrate.

The Golden Nuggets are broken down into four sections:

- What You Don't Know Can Hurt You
- All About Writing...
- The Whole Purpose of Marketing
- Rants, Raves, & Caves.

If you want to be ordinary then these gems are not for you. It doesn't take much to be ordinary–just be like everybody else; write like everybody else, think like everybody else, and play it safe like everybody else.

These Golden Nuggets will teach you how to write fearlessly without worry of rejection, criticism, or some specific result. They are designed to make you Think Differently, spark new ideas and have a compound effect at the end.

You may at first see the Golden Nuggets as self-promotional, but they are tools, writing pieces designed to teach you real marketing skills. They will entertain, provide valuable information, evoke emotions, and provide a clear call to action. They will also teach you how to write short copy and steal attention from the competition. That's important especially in this day and time when people's attention span is short.

So sit back, kick your shoes off, get a glass of your favorite wine and let us take you on a ride where you can be whatever you want to be: Don't Write To Be Famous, Write Like You're Already Famous.

P.S. Jennifer and I would like to thank you for your purchase, and if you've received just one idea then write an Amazon review to help others make an intelligent buying decision.

If one idea can change the world, one idea could change your life.

One other thing–for a Limited Time Only: Sign-Up within 7 days from the purchase date of this book and receive a Free 15 minute Consultation–How to Automate your tweets and set up an automated scheduler like TweetJukeBox. Sign up and send proof of purchase. http://mlemont.com

******

Now my publisher is telling me that we have to take a commercial break to pay some bills so we will be back in 2 minutes 2 seconds to present what I consider to be the Crown Jewels of the book–The Golden Nuggets.

Recommended Books And Services Offered By The Authors

HTG100K Dare To 2B Great Series>>

How To Gain 100,000 Twitter Followers, Secrets Revealed An Expert

Shorter Sampling Version

The Twitter Secret Key Revealed

Jennifer Lopez–

Online Spanish Coaching & Corporate Language Training Sessions

M LeMont–

Twitter Consultations and Marketing Services

Section 2: What You Don't Know Can Hurt You

Everything you do is paid training for your life's ambition. ~

JOURNEY OF 50,000 WORDS

My writing goes against the grain, honest and somtcimcs raw–it's never boring and hardly ever inappropriate. And it stands out from the crowd.

NOW, do you really want to write a book with me?

Wait. Don't answer. Not yet.

HATERS will judge you and make you want to quit.

But, in the end, it will be worth it, and we might create something REMARKABLE.

Are you ready?

"Yes. I'm ready."

Let's go.

Golden Nugget #1

Sacrifices–Long Hours–The Grind

Reading Time: 2min 50sec

"Lately, you've been paying me no ATTENTION."

Well, shit I've been busy. You know??

"Can't you see that it's driving me crazy?"

Yea, and it hurts so bad when you say THINGS like that.

WAIT–take a MOMENT and listen.

I work my ass off to make a living. No time off–7 days. I don't eat; I don't sleep–no balance.

Can't you see how you make me feel–you're slowly killin' me.

"Honey, I can't help it–I cry inside every time I hear your voice..."

Tell me, is this your version of support?

Then I don't want it anymore.

******

It took three marriages for me to realize why I was so selfish with my time. It was the bondage of trying to make someone else happy–the rules, and confinement and trying to live up to another's expectations.

The MINDSET of an entrepreneur is always: Work–Create things.

There's no Balance or Compromise when you're a CREATIVE person–either you Sacrifice the things you want to make someone else happy and suffer the pain yourself.

Or you selfishly pursue your goals and the other person grows to hate you for not giving them attention.

Yep, I've seen and done it all.

Do you hear me?

Now you can tell me to go take a hike but you still need to know.

The SACRIFICES and decisions YOU make to be a writer. The grind–long hours–and the people you hurt.

NOBODY understands.

IT TAKES COMMITMENT TO write every day.

How bad do you want it?

What are you willing to give up?

Who's going to get hurt?

One day, you'll have to make a decision whether you want to or not.

Are we clear?

Just think about it before you jump on the next train.

Comments: M LeMont, I hope you don't mind if I add my two cents. There are times when spouses, co-authors and loved ones disagree. This post was one of those moments for M LeMont and I as writers. We both understand the writer's creative, illusive mindset; the moments of sacrifice and the pain we cause loved ones when an inspired wave comes sweeping through our mind and we have to drop everything to write.

But experience can teach us to find balance and sacrifice in order to be our best self not only for ourselves but for the ones we love. In these moments, when we DO sacrifice–eventually the tide turns and comes back around to catch up with us again. We all have to make our OWN way through the Beautiful Mess of Contradictions. ~Jennifer

Golden Nugget #2

Why Loyal Followers & Fans Are Not Buying Your Ebook

Reading Time: 4min 2sec

If you're reading this article, I'm willing to bet that you're reading it on a mobile device, smart phone or tablet.

You're probably away from home, eating a meal, lying in bed, or standing in line somewhere.

People engage, communicate, and post using their phones and tablets more so than with their PC according to recent studies.

If you think that's good news you better keep reading.

More people access the Internet wherever they go 24 hours a day.

People are staying connected and are dependent on their mobile devices like bees are to honey.

1. More than seventy percent of Internet users access the Internet via mobile devices instead of a PC.

2. Mobile users spend more time on social media like Facebook and Twitter than any other social activity.

3. Mobile devices are being used for texting, email, research, maps, stocks, interviews, college courses, e-books etc.

Now that should be good news for authors–more mobile devices translate into more ebook sales, right? Wrong.

Less than 10% of mobile users have a Kindle. It means that 90% of your loyal followers and fans couldn't buy your e-book if they wanted to.

It also means 90% of people who click your links, read your blog, and click the Amazon link, can not buy your book.

Mobile users are unaware if they don't have a Kindle they can download a free app for their smart phone, PC, or tablet.

So everyone suffers from the lack of knowledge. And here's the next big problem. It took me 30 minutes to find the free Kindle app on Amazon–if you're not looking for it, it's easy to overlook.

If you want more e-book sales then you must educate everyone about the free Kindle app. Post the message below on your website and tweet it.

The links go straight to the Amazon page to download the free Kindle app. The process takes 1 minute. The app is sent to your email and then click the link to download. Done!

Twitter Comments: On June 18, 2015 @jonesythompson retweeted, "quick read that makes good sense."

Nick Spindler @nspindler, "I have a hard time believing people don't know about the app though."

I know, I was like everyone else, it's hard to believe. But that doesn't keep it from being true.

Copy the message below and put it on your website, tweets and book inquires.

Don't have a kindle? Download free app and start reading an ebook in 1 minute.

http://amzn.to/1BtVqdO

Golden Nugget #3

How to Find Market Mavens Who Write Quality Book Reviews.

Reading Time: 5min 2sec

If Social Media thrives on information then the person with the most information is the most important, the most respected and the one everybody listens to. They're called Market Mavens.

In Malcom Gladwell's book, The Tipping Point, he defines Market Mavens as information specialists who know 'their stuff' about products and services–a person who people listen to.

A Market Maven is socially motivated; they share their knowledge freely with friends, acquaintances or anyone who listens. They do this without charge or expecting anything in return, except the satisfaction of knowing that the information came from them.

I have a friend who's a Market Maven–he knows everything about stereo equipment and cars. He's obsessed with sharing this information to the point that it's all he talks about.

He's always on top of the latest information. But no matter how annoying he may get–when someone is in the market for a stereo...I refer them to him because I know he'll show them the best stereo, receiver and speakers on the market.

Then he'll tell them how to get the best price, buying it directly from the manufacture. He doesn't stop 'til he's sure they are informed and he's given them the telephone number and explain the warranty.

At one point, the manufacture even asked him to answer a few consumer questions because of his extensive knowledge of their product.

Market Mavens are like Santa's helpers in the market place–they help move products. They are part of the Universe's invisible sales force.

Okay, enough of all this crackling.

Where can I find these Market Mavens to review my book, you ask?

Alright, let me show you. And I'm sure some people already know this but there's a twist because I always see things differently, so stick with me, okay?

Look at Reviews of Competing Books. The Reviewers are already fans of that niche.

- Look for reviews that are long and detailed. Find those contentious reviewers that make you think, "Geez, I wish someone would write a review like that for my book."

- Click on the reviewers name to find their contact information: email address, website or Twitter handle.
- Only about 15% to 20% will have contact information. So, you'll have to dig to get your book in front of these people.

Market Mavens are not professional book reviewers and they are not raving fans–they are regular people like you and me. They are obsessed with writing and sharing their knowledge. They love being a top reviewer.

They also have many people who follow them and respect their opinions. They write long and detailed book or product reviews, blogs, and tell their friends on Facebook, Twitter, and book clubs–all for the satisfaction of helping other people know about your book.

Don't believe me? Here are two comments taken from a competitive book review regarding a Market Maven's review.

Mark D. Worthen says:

Excellent review! You probably didn't write the review for this reason (it seemed to be mainly to inform other Amazon customers and to express gratitude), but by being honest, personal, and by telling your story, you are creating a powerful brand for yourself. Thank you for your contribution.

Robert Morris says:

I greatly admire David Scott's reviews because they combine objective analysis of the given subject with provision of his own personal thoughts and feelings about it. That requires a delicate balance, which he consistently sustains.

Scott is a bridge builder between those who read his reviews and the books he praises. Some then journey across the bridge...others do not. That, in essence is what all reviewers struggle to be and do...and no one does it better than he does.

Get my point? Book Buyers love to read Market Mavens' book reviews.

Now the obvious thing would be to send these Mavens an Email, telling them how much you enjoyed their book review... and that you have a similar book you think they'd would enjoy reading. Then, you'd offer to send them a free copy.

Please, do me a favor–don't waste your Cotton Pickin time. They are not going to read your Freakin' book.

Market Mavens are bombarded with crap like that every day. Plus, you violated sales principles of this book:

1. Think Different and stand out from the crowd.
2. Sell your self and get people to like you, for YOU.

Here's what YOU SHOULD do instead:

- First, you're looking on Amazon for their Twitter contact information.
- Next, (and this is the only time)you'll send them an email, asking for that information AND letting them know how much you enjoyed their book review.
- Then, you tell them you'd like to follow them on Twitter and ask for their handle.

Now the fun begins.

If you have 100,000+ Twitter followers or a lot more followers than they have, they are going to view you as an influencer and be honored to follow you back.

Then you can build a relationship and over time they will be glad to review your book! Now that's a THINK DIFFERENT CROWD...WIN- WIN situation. Favor for favor, right?

You should follow at least 4 Market Mavens a month and focus on building relationships with them.

Alright, that's it from here–another Think Different strategy that works. Cheers!

Comments: If you have questions or comments about How to get Market Mavens to review your book drop me an email. Click here MLemont.com Hit the Contact us Button

Golden Nugget #4

More Bang for Your Bucks

Reading Time: 3min 12sec

This book is 348 pages and you should expect it to increase over-time.

The reason, you ask?

VALUE.

I like adding value to the already rich content–it separates me from the competition.

Plus, that's what you want, right?

More BANG for your Bucks?

Well, it's what you should do with your readers, give them more than what they expected.

I mean, OVER THE TOP, MORE.

Now let me have your attention for a moment.

Did you know that you can use Amazon's Automatic Update feature to offer free updates to your book?

When readers turn on this feature they receive automatic updates. The bummer is– you can't expect Amazon to send email notifications for book updates. So if you've finished reading a particular book, you'd likely never know if or when new content was added.

Well, this gives you–as an author–the opportunity to create a bond with your readers by advertising in the back of your book about the Auto Feature and UPDATES.

Plus, if you sell a How-To-Book, you understand that information is constantly changing. Your readers NEED to know WHEN you've discovered a new idea or if something is no longer working.

Here's how to turn on Amazon's Auto Update Feature:

- Go to your Amazon.com account
- Click on 'My Account'–at the top right corner of the page.
- Click: Manage Content and Devices
- There is a Horizontal Menu Bar at the top right–Click on 'Settings' on the far right
- Scroll down and turn on Automatic Book Updates. Done!

Now, if you want to be notified of updates to THIS book, simply Sign-Up and I'll send you an email anytime a major update is made. Otherwise, when you turn on the 'Auto Book

Update' Feature, you'll never know that you have updates or how to find them. In the email, I'll tell you what the update is and how to locate it.

By the way, I don't sell your private information or spam people with solicitations–that's just not my style. You'll get the updates when available and I'll go about my business.

Anyway, if you want More Bang for Your Bucks, sign up here: MLeMont and click on the blue Contact button and reference free updates. http://mlemont.com

Look, if you Sign-Up during the first 7 days of your purchase, I will give you these 2 extra bonuses:

–a private 15minute consultation via Twitter DM–How to Automate your Twitter account & Schedule Tweets, to become more effective.

And, when you buy Book 1, How To Gain 100,000 Twitter Followers, I will also give you a 15 minute consultation on how to gain followers using Twitter–in just 15 minutes a day.

Here's the link again, MLeMont

http://mlemont.com

Send purchase receipt and get the two extra bonuses–Kindle & Amazon Prime Members, also qualify.

Do it now, like your SUCCESS is riding on it. Who knows, it just might be.

Okay, I've gotta go and write the next Golden Nugget. Cheers!

P.S.

My email if you prefer:

bob@mistersalesman.com

Golden Nugget #5

The Best Kept Secret On Kindle

Reading Time: 3min 30sec

What if I told you that you had a big problem when a prospect clicked your Amazon book link and they received a message–this message:

"This book you searched is not available in your country."

Would you believe me?

Well, that's what's happening to many of your prospects that live outside of your home country.

I discovered this problem when a Twitter follower tweeted, "I tried to buy your book but it's not available in India."

Panic mode: What the shit is he talking about?

I immediately went to Google Search and found the URL for AmazonIndia.com and noticed that it was in US currency. The network was recognizing my IP address. That wasn't going to work, but I sent it to him anyway.

Now stick with me, if you're an author– you need to know this.

The prospect tweeted back and said thanks for the link, I bought the book. But it still didn't make sense.

So I researched and found that Amazon had 15 different individual country codes and you could only make a purchase using the correct code.

Now that was a huge problem. I'd been using the wrong URL. But how could I use 15 URL country codes in a tweet or on my website?

The Hunt For A Solution

After extensive research, I found a Universal link that connected all of Amazon Country codes into 1 link Booklinker.net.

"Every BookLinker URL is "Universal" and automatically takes readers to your book in their correct Amazon storefront. This means less barriers between your readers and purchasing your books."

You can even create custom or vanity links to share on social media and websites just like this one I created for my bestseller Twitter book:

http://getbook.at/HTG100K

Click and see where it takes you. The app also keeps record how many times the link has been clicked and lists them by country.

As you can see below, I've received 2,569,859 since September 2015 to March 2016.

Now for all you math geniuses correct me if I'm wrong, that's 428,309 hits a month or 14,276 per day that are going straight to my Amazon page.

Where are all those hits coming from?

Well, we'll talk more about that later, right now if you have a book on Amazon then you need more exposure–jump over to Booklinker.net and set up your free account.

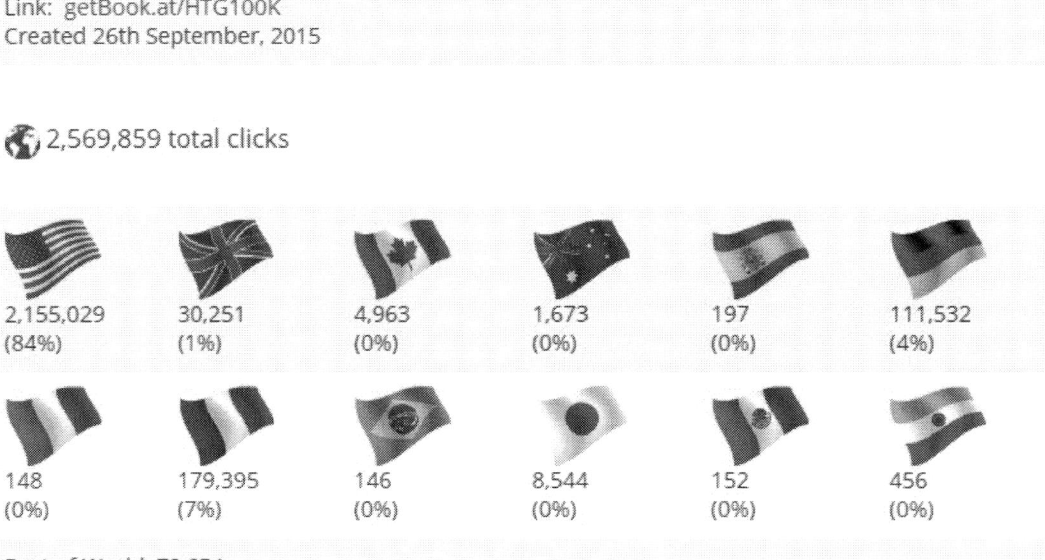

Golden Nugget #6

Bots Are Skewing Web Stats

Reading time: 2 Min 2 Sec

I'm sure you've seen ads how to get gobs of traffic to your website or landing page. As a matter of fact I've received two here recently. One was from a follower on Twitter and it said,

How I got 6.2 Million Pageviews and 144,920 Followers Google search headline

It's an excellent article about a mile long, but nevertheless, it contains some useful information.

Now I can go along with the 144,920 genuine followers, but the 6.2 million Pageviews is just as suspicious as my 2.5 million hits I had on my book link–I discussed in the previous chapter.

Then I received an email from a highly respected email marketer that said the results from his pay per click ads were off the chain, and in the last 30 days his ad was seen over 615,000 times and the last three days alone showed 165,879. (Sales were higher than they'd been in the last 30 days.)

Now there's no disputing sales figures that's for sure.

So what's my point? Sales figures don't lie but metrics do.

Bots are screwing up the numbers and if you are going to use hits as a primary measurement then you'd better factor in the Bot factor.

According to a 2013 study by Incapsula suggests 61.5% of all website traffic is now generated by bots. That was an increase of 21% from 2012 figure of 51%. And I'm sure today, the figures are much higher. That also means humans only account for 38.5% of Internet traffic.

Bot traffic is growing at an estimated rate of over 40% per year. It's costing advertisers millions of dollars in false metrics.

Now go ahead an say it... Okay, I'll say it for you... that's crazy as shit!

So what about the Booklinker.net Free app to track your Amazon book sales in real time? Well, if sales don't equate to the number of hits then you know 61% are bots hitting your link.

I created a Booklinker.net link for my book How To Gain 100,000 Twitter Followers on Sept 26, 2015 and by November 10, 2015, I had 756,951 click-thru to my Amazon book page. And on March 21, 2016 it increased to 2.5 million.

I also experienced a similar increase on my Amazon affiliate link of more than 400-500 a day generated from my website of daily visitors 500-600 which is an impossible click- thru rate. No matter how you look at it, the numbers don't add up.

Bots are created by companies and individuals for good and bad purposes.

The good bots gather consumer information for companies like Amazon, Google, Apple, and many others seeking consumer information.

Then there are bad bots that maliciously click on pay per click ads to skew the numbers and click on websites to steal information, or to increase fake traffic for the owners to show clients and get more ad revenue.

The Bottom line?

The only real measurement is "Frequency to Sales ratio." The number of times you tweet or run your ad compared with the number of sales. Sales don't lie.

Now, you can put things in the right perspective and not get so excited about web traffic. It's not as nearly as important as you think if you don't factor in the Bot.

And, by the way, you still need Booklinker.net because it's a Universal link for all of Amazon country codes, otherwise you'll be in big trouble.

P.S. Here's an update from Imperva:

When analyzing our data, we were very surprised to find out that, for the first time, humans were the ones responsible for the majority (51.5 percent) of all online traffic.

- *These numbers initially appeared to be a complete trend reversal. However, upon closer inspection, and when put in the context of our previous analyses, they actually signaled the continuation of a trend, which consists of:*

- *An increase in the relative amount of human traffic, from 38.5% in 2013 to 51.5% in 2015.*

  - *A decrease in the relative amount of good bot traffic, from 31% in 2013 to 19.5% in 2015.*

  - *A static amount of bad bot traffic, which fluctuates around 30%.*

Comments: Well, things improved but bad Bots are still messing up the numbers so just know that all web traffic, is skewed in one way or another. It will help keep a balance.

Golden Nugget #7

Hashtags Are The New SEO

Reading Time: 2min 2 sec

Hashtags allow you to categorize information so people can find it. If you are selling a product, add a tag to your tweet or headline.

Hashtags have become the new SEO.

People search Twitter and Google for information on anything and everything, using their favorite HASHTAGS.

When you add the # before a word like #SocialMedia, then anyone looking for topics on Social Media can find and click on the link.

Now here's the BIG little Secret.

Hashtags give you the ability to reach an entirely different market outside of the people who follow you. Think of each Hashtag as a market unto itself. People follow Hashtags like they follow people on Twitter.

Jennifer: What? Hashtags have their own followers?

M LeMont: Yes, in reality, you don't need any followers if you know the magic of Hashtags. But, if you did have a lot of followers it would expand your reach even farther.

Jennifer: This is intriguing. Why don't you give me some examples of a headline with Hashtags that you wrote...

M LeMont: Here's a tweet I wrote with plenty of Hashtags: **Make Your Tweets Stand Out.** getBook.at/HTG100K #Twitter #Authors #Writers #SMM #Ian1 #SocialMedia #SmallBitz #Marketing

Jennifer: How can I find out which are the most popular Hashtags?

M LeMont: Well, there is a special app I use that rates the popularity of Hashtags. Naturally you don't want to use a hash-tag with zero popularity because nobody's following those.

Go to: Hashtagify.me and type any word as a Hashtag. You want to use the Hashtags with highest ratings from the site: those with a score of 50 and higher.

Jennifer: That is a critical piece of marketing information ML, and I see why you use as many Hashtags as Twitter's 140 characters will allow.

M LeMont: The so-called experts will tell you not to use any more than 2 Hashtags because it looks ugly. Well, ugly stands out in the world of beauty.

Plus, each Hashtag is like a separate tweet. For example, if I use 5 Hashtags, that is equivalent to sending 5 additional tweets–in the same message.

I hope everyone got that?

I'm doing my best to break it down and show how important it is to Think differently about Hashtags. It's critical if you want to reach a larger and diverse market.

Jennifer: I want to go to Hashtagify.me right now to see how many people are in the #ThinkDifferentCrowd Hajajaja! Thanks M LeMont! You definitely have us Thinking Differently about the importance of Hashtags!

Golden Nugget #8

38 Most Commonly Used Hashtags

Reading Time: 2min 2 sec

1) #MustRead
2) #Fiction
3) #Non-Fiction
4) #BookGiveaway
5) #GoodRead
6) #FridayReads
7) #AmReading
8) #RomanceWriter
9) #SciFiChat
10) #Authors
11) #RWA (Romance Writers of America)
12) #IndiePub
13) #SelfPub
14) #SelfPublishing
15) #BookMarketing
16) #Ebooks

17) #Publishing

18) #GetPublished

19) #AskEditor

20) #AskAgent

21) #Ian1 (Independent Authors Network)

#Hashtags for Writing, Advice, Ideas, and Collaborate:

22) #AmWriting

23) #Grammar

24) #WritingTips

25) #WritingTip

26) #Writing

27) #WriteTip

28) #WriteChat

29) #NaNoWriMo (National Novel-Writing Month)

30) #SmallBitz

31) #Twitter

32) #SEO

33) #Marketing
34) #Sales
35) #SocialMedia
36) #SMM
37) #Digital
38) #Internet

Golden Nugget #9

How To Find Quality Followers?

Reading Time: 3min 10sec

Quantity first, then quality. When it comes to Social Media, the key element is 'MORE'.

You need MORE of everything.

MORE Disruption and MORE Disturbance. In order for a tropical storm to develop into a hurricane, it needs MORE wind, temperature, velocity, ease of flow and "The Butterfly Effect–the unknowns that makes it EXPLOSIVE!

Likewise, when you hit 100,000 Twitter Followers, something MAGICAL happens...

The Law of LARGE Numbers kicks in–a large number of followers attract MORE followers, MORE opportunities, MORE influence, MORE visibility, and MORE reach.

Now stick with me, I'm going to tell you a Secret that 99% of marketers don't know and if they do know, they're not telling anyone.

When I was approaching 200,000 followers, I knew it was time to drill down and find my target audience.

There's nothing better than having followers who are qualified to buy your product. It's like fishing in the right pond where the fish bite.

Since I sell books, I needed to find prospects that met certain criteria. So I used a strategy from my book How To Gain 100,000 Twitter Followers to find prospects who are:

- avid book readers
- prospects who owned tablets
- subscription based and bought books online from traditional book publishers.
- like @simonschuster who offers a free ebook for signing up on their mailing list.

Simon & Schuster have over 600,000 Twitter followers, and the HTG100K strategy is to copy @simonschuster followers.

Yes, you heard that right! Follow the same followers who follow @simonschuster and other book publishers.

I knew if I followed the strategies outlined in my HTG100K book, 50-60% of their followers would follow back.

Now I can add qualified prospects–increase my book sales and continue to grow my followers to the moon.

Would something like that work for you? Of course, it can but you want to make sure you're at Critical Mass before you drill down for Qualified Prospects otherwise you could fail miserably at both.

It took me 11 months to gain the first 100,000 followers and 12 months to gain another 100,000. If you want to learn more, go here:

getBook.at/HTG100K

Ps. My product guarantee: If you don't get amazing results in the first 48 hours, then lunch is on me. Oh, that's not good enough? What else can I give you? Okay, I hear you loud and clear.

I'll give you a free 15 min consultation–make sure your results in the first 48 hours are incredible and make sure you're on track to gain 100,000 Twitter followers.

How's that? Then get your booty on over to Amazon and download the book and send me proof of purchase Mlemont.com Cheers!

Golden Nugget #10

The Cash Cow: Recycle & Repurpose

Reading Time 2min 22sec

What are you doing with your old and forgotten blog posts or articles?

If you're like most bloggers–you archive the old and promote the new. Your best content could be buried under piles of other posts, and that's a good reason you should recycle them.

Recycle & Repurpose

The average shelve life of a post is a week or until you decide to write another one. But when you recycle it **'Consistently'** on Twitter, you extend its life.

I hate to repeat myself, but if I don't, you'll surely miss it. *The key word is to recycle, and promote the posts 'Consistently' on Twitter.*

For example, if you have a post that draws 500 views a month, then you've got a winner–a CASH COW that brings prospects through the door.

When a prospect reads 5 of your posts, then there's a good chance they'll buy something because they feel like they've bonded with you and you're no longer a stranger.

Content that's rich with solutions, that educates, and entertains can lead to MORE sales without making a direct pitch–simply by providing a link at the end of every post.

Repurpose Existing Content

Bloggers are content producers and can also repurpose their content into different marketing pieces and media channels such as Podcasts, Youtube videos, and ebooks.

What most writers fail to realize–it's never the post that makes the money–it's the ideas behind the post that ring the register.

Now, go and dig, in your archive, and find your long forgotten blog posts and recycle, and repurpose and promote them.

Customers are waiting on you.

Golden Nugget #11

No Hook, No Book

Reading Time: 2min 30sec

An eye-catching book cover, tile and subtitle are like sweet music to my ears. No Hook, No Book.

One of the first things that a songwriter creates is a hook in the melody, to make a song memorable to sing or hum.

Now that's the same thing you should do when writing a book. The content must contain hooks that can be used for the title, theme and marketing.

No Hook, No Book.

Did I ever tell you the fatal mistake Napoleon Hill almost made with his first published book?

Okay, I'll tell you now.

Well, originally the book Think and Grow Rich was going to be titled, 'Use Your Noodle to Win More Boodle'.

Yea, I know! What in the hell was he thinking, right? But a last-minute decision saved him from sure disaster that even his 13 Steps to Success probably couldn't have saved him.

Thank God, he changed the title to THINK And Grow Rich, because it captivated the world and created many millionaires.

The first thing prospects see is either your cover or the title of your book. Both are hooks that create an appetite to want to know more.

So, finding the perfect title is crucial. Look within the book itself, before you go searching your brain for something new. The title is probably buried deep inside a line.

If your book could talk, it would scream, "It's right here, use this sentence or use this phrase!"

Your title should be short & catchy so it will stand out. Your subtitle should be long enough to describe briefly what the book is about.

Jennifer and I were originally going to title this book, Don't Write To Be Famous, Write Like You're Already Famous. Then, at the last minute we decided the title was too long. So we shortened it to: ***Write Like You're Already Famous***. Fewer words create more impact and grab attention.

We also designed a cover of a woman looking fearless and confident attitude along with the subtitle, "Think Differently and Leave the Competition Standing in the Dust"–the theme of our book and a great marketing piece.

Here's the Bottom line. Write with the intent to create hooks within your book and understand the effect it will have on people. No Hook, No book. (Now that's a hook, I hope you remember.)

Golden Nugget #12

Looking for Mr. Goodbar

Reading Time: 3min 2sec

What's a nice girl like you doing in a place like this? Oh, you're Looking for Mr. Goodbar?? Honey, you seem like a good person with a good heart, but you're not going to find Mr. Goodbar in this noisy bar. There's nothing here but a lot of RIF RAF. ~1975

Well, the book Looking for Mr. Goodbar was published over forty years ago and things have changed quite a bit since then.

On-line book browsers search for books by typing keywords in Amazon search engine.

And if your book is not on the first page of search results, you run the risk of drifting into artistic oblivion no matter how good your book or writing skills.

I don't want that to happen to you. So here are *3 Powerful Secrets About Using Keywords*, listen carefully.

#1 Amazon allow you to use 7 keywords phrases that will help browsers find your book.

Log on to your Kindle account and click on the tab "Bookshelf". Then go to line item 3. Target Your Book to Customers Categories. Scroll down to the box titled Search keywords (up to 7, optional)

Here you will enter 7 keyword phrases that customers use to find your book. Enter each phrase with commas between phrases. For example, *how to get followers, how to use twitter.*

Once you enter the keywords they will be embedded in Amazon's search engine so think like book browsers–what phrase would they use to find your book?

Don't worry it will be difficult to get it right the first time around–you can always change them later.

A good idea is to ask customers what keywords they used to find your book, and then change your keywords.

Track and monitor your ranking on Amazon by typing in the keywords in Amazon search box to find your book the same way browsers search.

The combination of sales and hits on your keywords will move your book up the page ranks. This process could take a few weeks or a few months to get on page 1.

But no matter how long it takes you must continue to work until you get on Page 1 or your sales will suffer if nobody knows it exists.

2. Title of Your Books: If your title contains some of the same keywords, then you will move up the page rank faster as Amazon algorithms are designed to score higher for multiple keyword sources.

3. Description Page–When you write your description page make sure to add some of the same keywords into your copy. This will also score a higher page ranking with multiple keyword sources. Go to my Amazon description page How To Gain 100,000 Twitter Followers to see how I incorporated these 7 keywords in my description page. *how to get followers, how to use twitter, twitter for beginners, twitter for dummies, Twitter for writers, get more twitter followers, Twitter for authors.*

Now let me tell you something–just because someone found "Looking for Mr. Goodbar", it doesn't mean they were looking for it. Chances are they found it by accident and it could have been your book if you play your cards right.

So parallel–double park it side ways, and let them find you.

Golden Nugget #13

The Secret to Writing an Amazon Description Page

Reading Time: 2min 37sec

I study a lot of Amazon Description pages, and there's a good chance if you are in a genre I have also chosen to write in, I've studied yours.

Well, I'm sad to say that most of these description pages don't adequately describe what the books are about.

That's a BIG PROBLEM where I come from. There are HEAVY CONSEQUENCES–No Sales.

If people don't have an accurate description of what your book is about then, your fancy cover and title don't mean JACK–and I don't mean Jack-n-the-Box.

Your description page is a SALES AD and should not be dull and boring. It should motivate the prospect to hit that buy button or LOOK INSIDE your book.

Now, I admit writing a description can be a challenge, and hiring a copywriter is Expensive. So what should you do?

Draw Close and Listen:

I want you to FAKE IT until you make it.

Quentin Tarantino said, "I steal from every movie ever written, and if you don't like it I could care less, watch another movie."

Now, I want you to be that ideas person–but in this case I mean–GO GET the ideas and inspiration from OTHER Bestseller books description pages in your genre that EXCITE you. The ones that make you WANT to HIT the BUY button or look inside their book.

Yes, the great ones STEAL ideas and inspiration from each other. So join the club.

So study the description pages of the competition. It will get you inside the marketing departments of the best publishing houses in the country. Study things like: Headlines, Power words and phrases, Bullet Points, Layout and Structure.

Comments: Study bestselling authors description pages–they have huge marketing departments writing for them. Don't be afraid to steal an idea by rearranging word phrases. Remember there is nothing new under the sun!

Golden Nugget #14

How To Use Amazon "Look Inside" Feature To Make More Sales

Reading Time: 4min 5seconds

When it comes to selling e-books no company does it better than Amazon. It has enough intelligence information on book shoppers that it would make Homeland Security nervous.

For example–the "Look Inside" feature is where a browser can read the first 10% of your book, free.

It's your last chance to make a sale before they move on to greener pastures.

Amazon know that shoppers purchase books on 100% impulse and they also change their minds on the same impulsive behavior.

The Shopping Cart Abandonment rate for e-books is 70%.

Ouch!!! You got the customer to the table; the ink pen is in their profitable little hands, and they changed their mind at the last second.

What happened?

Well, maybe you bored them to death with all the dull information you put in front of your book; the

Acknowledgement page, sign-up for free newsletter, other books by author, dedication, disclaimer, and copyright.

Each turn of the page takes the shopper further away from hitting the buy button.

"And yes, all of this is your fault, so put that coffee down!"

COFFEE'S FOR CLOSERS.

I'm here to show you how to use the "Look Inside" feature.

It's your last good chance to land the sale before the shopper buys my book that Amazon advertised at the bottom of your description page.

I'm not going to bore them to death with a lot of excessive, wasted, and boring details.

When the shopper "Looks Inside" my book I'm going to take them straight to–Why I Wrote This Book, What They Can Expect, and The Table of Contents.

Now they can browse the chapter titles that I so perfectly selected and titled to be read in the first 10% of the book. This will help an undecided shopper who was straddling the fence, make a decision to buy.

The "Look Inside" is just as important as writing your book, so take it seriously.

So my sweet dumpling, here are **8 Ways To Use The "Look Inside"** feature to sell more books.

1. Plan and write the best material you can and place it in the front of your book.

It's like a sales letter, but you're not trying to sell them–customers don't want to be sold, they want to buy, and they don't want to be bored.

2. Don't put long & boring narration in the first 10% of your book. Put your best scenes first. Don't tell them–show them. Open the door–let them come in, and see the fight.

3. At the bottom of your DESCRIPTION page, add this note:

"Look Inside" Read 10% free. Scroll up to the top left corner of the page.

It's your last shot, so why not use it? Go to Amazon and take at the "Look Inside" feature in my book How To Gain 100,000 Twitter Followers and see how I added it to the bottom of my DESCRIPTION page. I'll wait right here until you get back.

4. Put all front material in the back of your book: Acknowledgements, Disclaimer, Newsletter, Dedication, Other books, Cover designer, Copyright, etc.

5. When the shopper "Looks Inside" quickly take them to the Introduction that you specifically wrote to motivate them to buy your book or at least to read The Table Of Contents.

I take the shopper directly to three pages titled:

- Why I Wrote This Book
- What You Can Expect From This Book
- Table Of Contents

Carefully name your Chapter titles and place them strategically in your Table Of Contents.

Go read the first 10% of your book on Amazon and see if it motivates you to buy it.

If the first 10% didn't motivate you to buy your own book, then rewrite the first 10% and make it better. Then publish the changes on Amazon. What? You can't make your book better because it's already published?

Who told you that? You can edit after publishing and even write more pages. It's a digital book, remember?

It will give you an enormous advantage.

The "Look Inside" feature is your last good chance to close the sale.

Don't think the shopper will come back later to make the purchase.

It doesn't work that way. If you only knew what a shopper is THINKING–you would be shocked!

Now go and make the changes. I bet a shopper is "Looking Inside" your book this very second.

Golden Nugget #15

Taking It To The Streets

Reading Time: 2min 2seconds

If you know how people buy books then you would know how to market them. I wanted to know, so I took it to the streets.

For 12 solid months, when customers told me about the fantastic results they were getting from How To Gain 100,000 Twitter Followers, I would ask the Million Dollar question: How did you find the book?

The Customer responses were very enlightening:

1. Amazon Keyword Search

2. By Category Listing on Amazon

3. Amazon–Readers Who Bought This Item also Bought this Book.

4. I was Browsing through a Kindle List on Amazon.

5. I typed your name into Amazon via Direct Search Engine.

6. I saw your tweet in #SocialMedia

7. I saw one of your posts on Google Search engine.

8. Your book & link were listed on another author's website.

9. My book club recommended it.

10. A friend had it on her Kindle app.

11. I saw a funny headline with your book link that caught my eye.

12. I received an email from Amazon and your book was on their Recommended List.

13. I read one of your blog posts.

14. I kept seeing pictures of frogs in my Twitter feed

15. I don't remember, but I'm glad I found it.

Those are the invisible forces that are going on behind the scenes that you can't see and don't know about.

The Bottom line? Create massive activity– disrupt and stir things up.

And the more followers you have, the more you can move fast and market faster.

Go here:

getBook.at/HTG100K

Golden Nugget #16

Finding Treasure Deep In The Amazon

Reading Time: 2min 30sec

In the Direct Mail Business, your success hinges first on a good mailing list. The ideal list has prospects who've purchased a product through mail order recently and done it more than once; especially those paying a high price for the product.

Plus, the mailing list itself is even better if it worked for other mailers with similar products.

Now a mailing list like that could make you a fortune–if you're just a half-way decent writer. But don't get excited because many mailing lists don't work anyway.

The same is true on the Internet. There are many companies, offering to promote your product through Pay-Per-Click Ads. But these prospects are a mixed bag of sorts, like getting names out of a phone book or using Google Pay-Per-Clicks. And many of those promotional claims, don't work–for whatever the reason. Maybe just too broad an audience with those not interested in what you're selling.

But there is one company that has an ideal prospect list: Amazon.com. This company has more than 240 million credit card customers on file and is the **perfect place to promote your books.**

You'll find prospects who:

- are searching to buy a book right now
- have a Kindle or Ebook Reader
- probably bought books before on-line
- bought a similar book recently
- are looking to buy in a particular genre

Amazon "pay-per-click" promotion is a treasure map to finding gold!

My dear reader, are you listening to me?

I'm trying to give you more AMMO for your repertoire.

You can set an ad campaign with a monthly budget as low as $100 and only pay when prospects click on your ad.

It will take them directly to your Description page. So, MAKE SURE your 'DP' and the 'Look Inside' are well written to motivate the prospect to hit that buy button.

Just follow these 4 simple and easy steps:

- Go To Kindle Publishing: Right next to the cover of your book,
- Click Promotion and Advertise.
- Set your budget and criteria.
- Monitor, track results, and make adjustments–write a new ad or change categories until you get the desired results.

Comments: Although Amazon "pay-per-click" may not work for everybody, it's what you're supposed to be doing–promoting your books for more exposure and action. There is no better platform than Amazon. Social Media demands Massive Exposure through multiple channels, so find them and use them.

Golden Nugget #17

Why the 0.99 cent Book Selling Strategy Sucks

Reading Time: 3min 33sec

There was a time back in 2010 when the 0.99 cent book selling strategy worked like a charm.

During that time John Lock, the King of 0.99 cent books, became famous and sold millions of copies. But now everyone is doing it and there's a glut of books on the market at that price point.

It's a matter of supply and demand.

Everyone wants to sell on price and not on content.

That idea's a FLOP because it devalues the worth of all e-books.

I currently have 7 books published: my novels are priced at $3.99 and non-fiction books priced at $4.99 and $9.95.

The Grind, the Work and the Sacrifice that go into writing a book and then selling it for 99 cents, oh makes me nauseous just to think of it. The royalties 70% or less (depending on Country) equate to almost nothing.

Now I'm an author and I love what I do, but I didn't become published to do charity work.

What about you?

So why are authors selling at this price point? Well, let's take a look.

Potential Advantages-selling at 0.99 cents

1. It promotes sampling of an author's books at little risk to the customer.
2. It encourages impulse buying, what buying things on the Internet is all about.
3. More sales can increase Amazon ranking.
4. More book reviews

Disadvantages

1. There's a good percentage of the market who associate a low price point with crappy books. Perceived value means everything.

Imagine if I sold my Bestseller: HTG100K for 0.99 cents? The Twitter secrets would have a **perceived value of zero**. The book sells for $9.95 and the price alone says that it contains valuable information.

My book wouldn't stand out on price from the rest of the 4,000 Twitter books if I sold it for 0.99-$2.99.

2. Once someone buys your book at 0.99 cents, you are conditioning them to expect to buy all your books at 0.99 cents. And if you sold your future books for a higher price, some folks would think they were getting ripped off.

Plus, the 0.99 cent strategy can have negative consequences.

3. Reviews–You would think you would get more reviews selling at 0.99 cents, right? Wrong! They bought your book because of impulse buying; the title looked interesting, and the cover grabbed their attention. It was a bargain. But here's the real deal. They also bought a lot of other books for 0.99 cents and even downloaded a shit load of books for free.

4. Fans–There are very few loyal fans who buy books at 0.99 cents. To them, it's all about price.

The 0.99 cent strategy can have negative consequences.

Here's what one reviewer had to say about a famous author's book he was displeased with. Notice the huge gap between price points.

"I should have known when his fiction was 99 cents and this one was $5 that I was being played for a sucker."

So where's your book in the hundreds of e-books on their Kindle? WHEN will it get read?

I hope you see what I mean here!

Don't believe me? Try raising the price of your next book from 0.99 cents to $3.99 and see how many of those loyal fans would buy. The 0.99 cent crowd follow the price and not the content.

Golden Nugget #18

Why You need a Table Of Contents Strategy

Reading Time: 2 min 2sec

When I published my first book The Point of No Return, I did not have a Table Contents (TOC) nor a Table of Contents Strategy. Like so many authors I didn't know the importance of having one, nor how to create it.

Then one day, I got an email from Amazon that said I was missing a Table of Contents and went on to explain that,

"A Table of Contents provides readers with both easy navigation and improved visibility into the contents of the book."

I now include one in every book I write.

Shoppers look at 4 things before buying a book: cover, title, book description, table of contents.

A lot of careful thought should be given to the headings and layout of your Table of Contents.

Think of the TOC as a sales letter or an ad in the newspaper. It's that important.

It gives readers a quick glance inside your book and helps them make an intelligent buying decision.

Take a quick glance a the Table Of Contents for the first 10 chapters of this book and you'll see what I mean.

Now, I'm going to take away the excuse–I don't know how to create a Table of Contents.

Read the next Golden Nugget and I'm going to show you how to create a workable TOC.

Golden Nugget #19

How to Create a Workable Table of Contents

Reading Time: 2min 2sec

Here are 10 easy steps to create a workable Table of Contents if you are using Windows 7 and above.

When creating a Table of Contents it should be the last thing you do before publishing your book.

1. The first step is to create a new page in the front of your book and type Table of Contents.
2. Now go to each chapter and highlight or drag your mouse across the Chapter Heading.
3. Then find your Style tab at top of your menu bar scroll down and click on Heading 1.
4. Now highlight and do each chapter the same way, so Microsoft Word can locate and create your Table of Contents by keyword Heading 1.

5. Now you're ready for Microsoft Word to locate the chapter headings that you've highlighted with Heading 1 and create your Table of Contents.

6. Go to your Table of Contents page you created and place your cursor below the Table of Contents heading where the table contents will appear.

7. At the top of your screen you pull down the tab "Insert" it's between the View and Format tabs. Windows 7

8. Click on Reference

9. Click on Index and Tables

10. Click on Table of Contents

11. Unclick the two boxes that show page numbers and right align page numbers

12. Click the box use Hyperlinks instead of page numbers

13. Show levels Click on Level 1, Header 1 will appear at the top right of screen.

14. Hit the okay button and if all went well, Whola! You have a workable Table of Contents.

Now if everything I just showed didn't work then here's an excellent tutorial video by Tom Corson-Knowles that will give you a visual. Pc users hold down the control button and click the link or type the URL http://bit.ly/1EWkpgh .

Golden Nugget #20

Why You Should Post-Edit Your Books

Reading Time: 2min 2sec

"What! Post edit? I'm not suppose to do that. Who said I could? I feel bad. I've done everything I could to publish error free, and I'm disappointed. How many did you find?"

I said, "No worries, you can fix them."

"No, it's too late. I'll just let them be. I won't bother."

It was apparent that she was under some notion or potion that you shouldn't fix typos and errors after publishing your book.

But what was more alarming she had a closed mind and wasn't part of the new Think Different Crowd. (TDC), where you exploit and break the rules whenever you can gain an advantage.

And this was a golden opportunity because most authors don't post-edit their books. And it's for two reasons; psychological and know-how.

Now let me remind you, we live in a digital age, so you don't have to get it right the first time. Having the ability to make changes to your book after it's published is a good thing.

I normally publish two days before the release and buy a copy, read it and fix errors and then republish. And I'll keep doing things to my book long after publication if it makes it better.

Think about all the thousands of readers who haven't bought your book yet.

So take the shackles off your mind, it doesn't have to be "politically correct."

We'll leave that to the poor souls who subscribed to that class.

Have you ever thought of a phrase or scene that you wished you had written in the original upload?

Let me give you an example: One of my followers retweeted an excerpt from my novel Shh! Kiss Me Baby with her comment:

"If I had the time I would give him a taste of what a real woman is and what his money can't buy."

Wow! That was hot and steamy. And six months later after the book was published, I added that line into my book. I'm always making my books better long after they are published.

So have no fear, you're part of the Think Different Crowd (TDC) go edit and make your book better.

In case you forgot, I'm going to show you how. Let's go to the next Golden Nugget.

Golden Nugget #21

Four Steps To Edit After Publication

Reading Time: 2min 2sec

Here are four steps to editing or rewriting after publication that I highly recommend to give you a competitive advantage.

And, by the way, if you don't know who the competition is–it's every author who has a book published on Amazon, especially those in the same genre as yours.

So you need all the help you can get and this is a Big one.

1. Make changes to your manuscript that was uploaded to Kindle.
2. Upload manuscript to Kindle the same way you did the first time you published it.
3. Upload completed–Click the Preview button and view your book on all Kindle devices to make sure changes are correct.
4. When you hit the publishing button, all changes will override the original book.

During the publishing process your book is still available for purchase. It takes 12-24 hours for your book to appear on Amazon.

That's it–it's that simple. Post-editing gives you a huge edge, but you've got to change your thinking.

Henry Ford said it like this, "If you think you can, and if you think you can't–you are right either way."

Golden Nugget #22

Automate Everything!

Reading Time: 2min 2sec

Smart people start a business on the Internet, Automate it–create a revenue stream and then move on to start another one.

If it can save you time, then find a way to automate it. Once you spend time, you can't replace it or buy more. It's gone.

I believe one day everything will be automated and that's the day the bots will rule.

After I hit 100,000 Twitter followers, I wondered what was next?

How could I take it to the next level?

How could I find more time to interact with my followers and provide consistent, solid and timeless articles that are always in season. Plus, ideas that would allow me to tweet more often and reach a larger audience.

The answer, in a nutshell is finding a way to automate everything and make it fun and entertaining: Tweets, Retweets, Curate Articles, Promotions, Direct Messages, etc.

There are several auto scheduler companies. I recommend TweetJukeBox.com because of its ease of use. It’s a no-brainer with TweetJukebox.com. Watch the tutorials and you'll see what I mean. Click here PC users hold down the Control button or copy URL into your browser.

https://youtu.be/8_9V-VTml6I

My second favorite is Hootsuite, which is also an excellent scheduler but a little bit more challenging.

Limited Time Only–Free 15 minute consultation:

How to use TweetJukeBox.com if you register the purchase of this book within the first week of your purchase. I will walk you through the process and give you some invaluable secrets that I've discovered. Name has changed to SocialJukeBox.com

Go to MLeMont.com click Contact and send proof of purchase.

P.S. Someone asked if we had a dog in this race. Absolutely not. We don't earn a commission for recommending either of those scheduling companies. Plus, we are offering the free consultation to show our appreciation for your purchase.

Golden Nugget #23

This is Water

Reading Time: 2 min 2sec

There are these two young fish swimming along, and they happen to meet an older fish swimming the other way, who nods at them and says, "Morning, boys, how's the water?" And the two young fish swim on for a bit, and then eventually one of them looks over at the other and goes, "What the hell is water?"

Now for the shocking answer, I want you to read the commencement speech by David Foster Wallace for Kenyon College. But I don't want you to read it now. I've included the link in the resource section of the book with a few other goodies for those who make it to the end.

What's that?

You want to read it now?

Are you sure it won't be a distraction?

Okay, then, let me say this first. The point of the fish story–"This is Water", is that the most immediate, obvious, ubiquitous and important realities are often overlooked by many. I know that may sound like abstract bullshit, but it's reality for 7 billion people.

On second thought, since I don't want you thinking like the rest of the world, it's a good idea to stop and read this article now. Google Search: There are these two young fish swimming along, and they happen to meet an older fish swimming the other way…

Golden Nugget #24

Why You Should Use Twitter Advanced Search

Reading Time: 2 min 2 sec

If you are looking for a way to increase sales, Advanced Search can locate and identify conversations about your product or industry. It is a highly-refined search compared to the regular Twitter searches that often return poor to no results.

Since writing the Bestseller, How To Gain 100,000 Twitter Followers–I search using the keyword phrase "how to use Twitter," and instantly find conversations related to my book.

Do you think that can help boost sales? You bet your booties, tootsies– it can.

10 Ways To Use Twitter Advance Search

1. How to locate your target market
2. Find customers talking about your product, genre or industry.
3. Look for (Buying Signals)
4. Discover competitor Tweets

5. Find GIF videos to entertain your followers
6. Find photos that relate to certain topics
7. Review your interactions with other people
8. Locate tweets for a specific geographic area
9. Search specific blogs to retweet
10. Follow people who are talking about your niche.

If you're in business, you can't do without Twitter Advanced Search

Golden Nugget #25

The Laboratory of Dreams for Creative People

Reading Time: 4min 40sec

Over the past year, I kept hearing the name FIVERR.com, but I never took the time to find out more.

Then one day, a highly influential person told me that he ordered a business logo from 3 different designers through FIVERR for $5.00 each, and they were professionally done.

He insisted that I look into FIVERR as both a buyer and seller.

So what is FIVERR? Well, first let me tell you what it's not. It's not like EBAY and it's not like AMAZON.

I bet if you asked 1,000 people what FIVERR was, you would get 1,000 different answers.

So, I'm going to break it down from two different perspectives–buyers and sellers.

Stick with me now, because I may exceed my 2 minutes 2 seconds–reading rule but it will be well worth your time.

From a buyer's perspective, FIVERR is where you go to buy products and services on the cheap from independent business owners who are trying to make a name for themselves.

Independent Business Owners are willing to sell a sample of their services for $5.00 and that may be all you need–the sample.

FIVERR give Sellers an opportunity to offer their products and services through a virtual marketplace.

And just like McDonalds $1 menu is designed for you to 'super-size' or add more to your order...

Sellers have extra gigs that can be added-on, to increase their profit.

For creative people who know how to use FIVERR, it's a laboratory of dreams where you can purchase virtually everything for any project.

I've purchased a wide range of products and services like: book covers, YouTube videos, story narrators, and advanced Excel templates for spreadsheets.

I'm excited about the FIVERR concept. So I joined as a buyer and a seller.

Whatever your dream, you can realize it on FIVERR.

If you have a special talent or skill–now is the time to launch that idea and become an Independent Business Owner. Or, fulfill your creativity needs as a buyer, and use Fiverr as your own personal Laboratory of Dreams.

To sign up as a buyer or seller is free.

Golden Nugget #26

Think Differently–Write Book Reviews on the Competition

Reading Time: 2min 2 sec

This is an actual review that I wrote on Amazon. Why did I write it? Well, let's see.

From time to time I like to see what the competition is doing, so I purchased the Best-Seller, The Art of Social Media, by Guy Kawasaki. It includes a wealth of information and power tips that generate an inexhaustible stream of ideas.

If you are a business owner and want to know how to promote your business and influence people on social media, then buy this book.

The title of the book makes one point exceptionally clear. Social Media is an art that must be learned, but I've also come to understand that Social Media is a science that must be understood.

The author provides many web links to "free" resources with information worth it's weight in gold.

The book is a quintessential blend of what works on Social Media and what doesn't. It is a treasure chest of one idea after another. A must read for any serious individual who wants to make a splash on the Internet. I rated the book 5 Stars.

Also, if you're wise enough to read The Art of Social Media and my latest book– How To Gain 100,000 Twitter Followers, you'll have knowledge that 99.9% of Internet users don't have. It's what I call an unfair advantage.

Now here are the reasons why you should Think Differently about writing reviews on the competition:

- You become a credible source for recommending books that contain valuable information to your followers. Who knows, you may even catch the attention of the author–especially if you add their Twitter handle to your tweet.

- You can promote the Review with a link to your website where you recommend both books side by side.

- You can nicely mention your book in the review on Amazon without a link.

- If enough people buy both books, your book could become associated with the Best-Seller and you might get on the Amazon list–**Customers Who Bought This Book Also Bought**... (yours)

- You keep a pulse on what the competition is doing, providing yourself inspiration and continued education.

Comments: Think differently and write reviews on famous authors who have similar books to yours. Promote them on Twitter every day in your automated system. Here's a peek at how I promote the reviews on my website The Art Of Social Media and how Jennifer promotes Collaboratives on her site. http://thejennieration.com/piealamode/

Break Time

Whenever someone says something is unfair–it means they are operating at a disadvantage. Your job is to keep the upper hand. Congratulations for reading this far. There is so much information it's easy to get overwhelmed, so let's take a quick 2min 2sec break before we go to the next section.

If you've learned even one idea you'll implement or if this book has made you think differently, then please take a moment and write a review on Amazon. It doesn't have to be anything fancy, but your review is valued by others who are looking to make an intelligent buying decision.

Here are some other books offered by M LeMont and services by Jennifer C. Lopez.

HTG100K Dare 2B Great Series

How To Gain 100,000 Twitter Followers, Secrets Revealed An Expert

Shorter Sampling Version

The Twitter Secret Key Revealed

Jennifer C. Lopez

theJennieration.com/translating-interpreting-services/

Spanish Mini-Tutorials Online w TheJennieration

Novels by M LeMont

Shh! Kiss Me Baby

M LeMont Caught Up What's Done In The Dark Comes To Light

Hot trailer over 2,000 views

Thank you for reading. Now let's return to the Golden Nuggets.

Section 3: All About Writing...

I THOUGHT just an invitation would have been fine, but I wouldn't have learned a damn thing. So be disruptive with me.

I will!

Don't get discouraged when someone tells you–your draft is a piece of shit. Instead, say–thanks...

I can FIX IT.

Now go and make it better. That's what becoming a GREAT writer is all about. And if you can't do that, then it's time to go the f... home.

Blessed are the Gypsies,

The Makers of Music,

The Artists, Writers,

Dreamers of Dreams,

Wanders and Vagabonds

Children and Misfits: For They

Teach Us To See The World Through

Beautiful Eyes.~Unknown

Golden Nugget #27

Write it Now and Sell it Forever

Reading Time: 2min 2sec

If you're a newbie and thought about writing a book, this piece is for you. And if you're not a newbie, there's still a lesson to be learned.

Everybody has a story to tell.

You've got a life, right?

Then you have a story, so why not tell it?

You don't have to use a lot of FANCY WORDS.

It's simple, write like you talk.

Like you're talking to a friend at the kitchen table.

Now don't tell me, you can't do that?

Okay, here's a pen and pad.

WRITE IT DOWN.

WRITE IT DOWN ON PAPER.

NOBODY NEEDS TO SEE.

NOBODY NEEDS TO KNOW.

How do you think J. K. Rowling, author of the Harry Potter series got started?

She sat down with an old typewriter in the face of adversity and typed her first words.

You can do it too. Write about your experiences–take all the boring parts out and you might have a Hollywood movie–who knows.

Write it Now and Sell it Forever.

If you want to know more go here: Write Like You're Already Famous

Comments: This is a post I run on Twitter every day. If you've always wanted to write a book but didn't know how to get started–now you know. Write it down–the first sentence is the hardest. Then keep writing. And if you're already an author–read the marketing piece again because it shows how to evoke emotions for a specific audience.

Whether you write fiction or non-fiction, your posts and ads should not be typical. Don't be afraid to be different–you're part of the Think Different Crowd. Also, notice the call to action at the end and how it relates back to a link for this book.

Golden Nugget #28

Rat Files–Who Took the Cheese?

Reading Time: 5min 2sec

Good writers are like Templeton the Rat, in the E.B. White's famous book, Charlotte's Web. **They KNOW how to take the cheese and run.**

In his book Steal Like an Artist, Austin Kelon said, "At some point an artist gets asked the question, Where do you get your ideas?"

The honest artist answers, "I steal them."

Some people collect art, gold and coins, but as a creative writer I collect things which are worth stealing–ideas, words, phrases, quotes, drawings, headlines, email subject lines, layouts or formats.

I collect them so I can reuse, reshape and remake them into something even more wondrous than the original....if there is such a thing.

In the publishing world, the best writers keep "Swipe Files," a collection of other people's works and ideas, which they use to be creative.

I prefer to call them "Rat Files," stealing the cheese and making THAT originality **MORE FLAVORFUL**.

Quentin Tarantino said, "I steal from every single movie ever made. I love it. If my work has anything, it's that I'm taking this from this and that from that and mixing them together. If people don't like it, then tough titty, don't go and see it, alright? I steal from everything. Great artists steal; they don't do homages."

Think Differently, The Best Artists Know How to Bring Life into Something that Already Existed!

"But I invented Twitter...." said Jack,"

"No, you didn't invent Twitter," Ev replied.

"I didn't invent Twitter either. Neither did Biz. People don't invent things on the Internet. ***They simply expand on an idea that already exists."***
~Hatching Twitter

History tells us that the best writers know how to find good ideas that already existed and make them masterpieces.

Shakespeare stole from the plays of the writers of his time: And so did Oscar Wilde, Thomas

Jefferson, Thomas Edison, Albert Einstein, Benjamin Franklin and many others.

The treasure lies in the ideas and works of others; it lights the spark for other artists to bring a full and brilliant flame of inspiration!

Many copywriters steal headlines from popular magazines like National Enquirer and Cosmopolitan Magazine and make them their own.

Listen!

Every idea emanates from another idea that came before it.

There is nothing new under the sun that has not been said or done before.

Every thought stems from a thought proceeding it; every word or sentence came from another word or sentence before it; and every idea, from another idea that previously sprung forth.

Every cell builds on another cell, and that cell doesn't care about originality.

Without life before, there would be nothing afterwards.

We are here because our parents came first, and their parents before them.

"What is Originality? Undetected plagiarism." ~William Ralph Inge

"Art is theft." ~Pablo Picasso

Woody Allen in all his unique, eccentric brilliance called himself, a shameless thief.

"Immature poets imitate; mature poets steal; bad poets deface what they take; good poets make it into something better, or at least something different. The good poet wields his theft into a whole feeling which is uniquely different from that from which it was torn." ~T.S. Eliot

You don't have to be the smartest person in the world to invent things. Look around you and make something aflame with your own creativity.

"The only art I'll ever study is stuff that I can steal from." ~David Bowie

When people call something "original" nine out of ten times they do not know the references or the original sources involved. ~Jonathan Lethem

Mark Twain said, *"It's better taking what does not belong to you, then to let it lie around neglected."*

So NOW, you get my point–it has all been used before.

"You can discover yourself, by copying the work of others and then finding yourself." ~Yohji Yamamoto

Jim Jarmusch said, "Steal from anywhere that resonates with inspiration or fuels your imagination. Devour old films, new films, music, books, paintings, photographs, poems, dreams, random conversations, architecture, bridges, street signs, trees, clouds, bodies of water, light and shadows. Select only things to steal from that speak directly to your soul. If you do this, your work (theft) will be authentic."

Francis Ford Coppola said, "We want you to take from us. We want you, at first, to steal from us because you can not steal. You will take what we give you and will put it in your own voice, and that's how you will find your voice, and that's how you begin. Then one day someone will steal from you."

Thomas Edison said, "The greatest inventor, is "Accident"

Okay, now you've heard it from the greatest poets, writers, and inventors the world has ever known.

What's the Bottom Line?

Think differently than the crowd and be like Templeton the Rat! Have at that Cheese, but give it some FLAVA!

Comments: Swipe a few good things every day and throw them in your Rat Files to use later: headlines, sentences, quotes, snippets from songs and movies, then rearrange and repackage them into something that looks, sounds and feels different.

Golden Nugget #29

Me & The Judge

Reading Time: 33sec

THE JUDGE SAID, "DO YOU SWEAR TO TELL THE TRUTH, THE WHOLE TRUTH AND NOTHING BUT THE TRUTH, SO HELP YOU GOD?"

I SAID, "HELL NO, I'M A WRITER!"

Don't Write To Be Famous, Write Like You're Already Famous.

Comments: That's a good example of what you can do with short and powerful words to grab attention. Make your reader smell, taste, and touch what you are saying. Less words=twice the benefit.

Golden Nugget #30

Should I Use Spanish In My Writing?

Reading Time: 2min 20sec

"Should I use Spanish in my writing –I don't want to alienate or offend my readers?"

Well...well, what do we have here? You're worried about alienating your audience when just the opposite is true.

Bring out the FLAVA, add a little spice.

Using Spanish in your writing can take an ordinary scene and make it memorable.

Just a little pinch adds lots of **FLAVOR**–and can make the reader smell, taste, and feel what you're saying. It's beautiful to see the words and translations side by side.

Here's a scene from one of my books, Caught Up where I used 1st Person POV and character dialogue to describe the setting and create a lot of tension.

It was a long walk back to the car. I noticed that we were being followed by a guy wearing shades and a sombrero. I didn't want to alarm Veronica–

so I said, "Hold on to your purse and bags tight, and most of all don't panic."

She said, "What's going on?"

"We're in the section of town called Little New York." Soon as I uttered those words, another guy appeared directly in front of us.

He said, "Hey Amigo, me and my friend, who's behind you, watched your car while you were shopping."

"Really? That was nice."

"Yes, Amigo, si a cuidarlo–to Keep it Safe."

"Since I didn't tell you to do that, how much are you going to pay me M...F****r before I kick your ass for touching my car. Una patada en el culo para tocar mi auto."

"Veronica, get in the car and lock the door."

Then, the other guy shouted, "Hombre you're F***ing lucky my vato is in a good mood–otherwise you would be un hombre muerto–Dead–man."

A little dash of Spanish is like 'spice' that draw readers into your story–it can intrigue and set the tone for rest of your book.

Your opening line must GRAB YOUR READERS, or they have no reason to read further.

Just like a good fight, READERS EXPECT YOU TO GRAB THEM.

So, Do It.

Just remember, your opening line buys you TIME, but minutes only. I can assure you– the momentum will die if you don't continue to BE CREATIVE.

Now I can't say any more than that.

So, go forth, interject a few Spanish words and Grab the reader. Grab their attention and keep them reading. ¡Aclamaciones! Cheers!

P.S. If you're curious how the opening line in my novel unfolded, watch the trailer on YouTube: Caught Up, What's Done In The Dark Comes To Light.

Golden Nugget #31

Without Listening Something Terrible Happens... Nothing!

Reading time 2min 2sec

A few years ago, I bought a wonderful little book: Listening for Success, by Steve Shapiro. After reading it, I realized–you can't become a great writer without being a great listener. The book is only 48 pages, but one of the most powerful books you'll ever read.

What is SUCCESS?

Everyone defines it differently, don't they?

Most people THINK that hard work will make you a success.

Well, I know many people that work hard and have never achieved it. You see, I can get a donkey to work hard, but I can't get him to do one thing that success demands…LISTEN.

Here Lies the Secret in a NUTSHELL.

It's embedded within the word itself

S-U-C-C-E-S-S.

- Simple
- Understanding

- Caring
- Concern
- Empathy
- Sincerity
- Sympathy

When you engage in a conversation make it simple and short, let the other person talk.

"Everybody wants to talk, and nobody wants to listen. It's human nature to want to talk, talk and talk... chopping people's words at the root before they speak. Even worse, often never hearing a word that was said– you were too busy thinking of what you were going to say next." ~Stephen Shapiro

Now tell me, how rude is that?

The treasure is in the conversation if you listen to learn.

Listen!

You can hear the birds sing, crickets chirp and dogs bark, but have you ever listened to what they're saying?

If you listen carefully, you know when they're hungry, sick, happy, sad or in danger.

You can do the same with people.

"If you love to listen, you will gain knowledge and if you incline your ear–you will become wise." ~Sirach

Listening is a form of communication and persuasion. It's a powerful tool in building relationships when you genuinely care.

Think about it…when was the last time you listened to your spouse, kids, prospects, friends, parents or employees?

I'm not talking about just hearing them in an artificial way. I'm talking about being present with them in the MOMENT and passionately listening to every word.

The lack of listening is the main cause of broken marriages and the country's high divorce rate. Somebody else listened to your spouse and you didn't.

Now take a moment and watch this Video, Google search: "It's Not About the Nail." This is so crucial I'm going to wait right here until you finish. (PC users hold down the Control button and click link.)

******

Listening is the biggest problem people have when trying to sell on the internet, because without it, they don't know their audience.

If you want to increase your sales, you must listen to what motivates your prospects to action.

You have to show people that you genuinely care through your writings and interaction.

People buy from people they like and have confidence in.

What about your doctor, does he listen to his patients?

There's a reason he has "Practicing" before the title, 'physician'. He doesn't know what's wrong, unless he listens to what you have to say. But not all doctors listen, do they?

Many deaths occur every year from misdiagnosis because someone didn't listen.

I know many of you right now are saying this is stupid. I don't have to listen to this crap.

Do you see what I mean?

You're not even listening to what I'm saying, are you?

God gave you two ears so you could listen twice as much.

He also gave you two arms, two legs, two eyes, two feet, two hands, so there must be a reason why he only gave you one mouth.

We live in a sin sick world:

- A troubled teen walks into an elementary school, shoots everyone in sight because his parents wouldn't listen when he was growing up.
- Wars are started because the leaders are not willing to listen. Where are the weapons of mass destruction?

Were they ever found?

Thousands of lives were lost because the leaders from both countries didn't listen.

What Room Would You Choose?

"If you had a choice of walking into a room where everyone was a genius except you and all you could do was listen, or a room where you were the smartest– which room would you choose?"

In which room do you think you would learn the most?

Of course, you would learn more in the room with the smart people–because you would be more inclined to listen.

However, in room #2 you could also learn but because you were the smartest, you would be too busy telling everyone what you know.

Bottom line?

You are going to be a great writer one day... when you **LISTEN MORE**.

Thank you for listening.

Comments: There is so much to write about all around us if we would just take a moment and listen. You can pick up a copy of Listen For Success by Stephen Shapiro –the book will help you THINK differently and give you an enormous edge over the competition. We do not receive any commissions on any book recommendations.

Golden Nugget #32

Fewer Words–More Impact

Reading Time: 2min 2sec

The majority of writers play it safe and write–thick and chunky content. But if you want to stand out from the crowd, learn how to use fewer words to draw the reader into your story.

Here's what I mean.

In walked a man, butt naked. I mean, not one stitch of clothes on.

"I need your clothes, your boots, and your motorcycle." [Everyone at the bar laughed]

And the guy said, "You forgot to say please." Then he stuck a burning cigar deep into the man's chest. Ouch! Why did he do that!

It was arm CRUSHING and head SMASHING time.

Meet the TERMINATOR! Now go, raise some hell!

That was a commercial from the new Terminator game. It's an excellent example of how to captivate an audience. Arnold Schwarzenegger illustrates that less is more–fewer words, MORE IMPACT.

You must hit the reader with a crushing opening line, short and snappy words, sentences and phrases.

Are we clear?

Maybe not?

Okay, here are a few ideas, and just by practicing them, it will give you an edge because the majority will not do them.

It's hard and too much work. But if you practice the right things every day it will get easier, and you will get good at it. So good that one day, people will scour their emails and Twitter page to read your content.

- Study and analyze the works of other writers, authors, screenwriters, movies, songs, poetry, commercials, actors, artists, etc. Look for uniqueness in style. Then copy it until it becomes your own.
- Practice writing 100 words every day; sharp, crisp and tight content and headlines.
- Repeat and tweet the same post every 4 hours. It's the same thing news stations do with their top news stories of the day. Less

than 1% of your followers are on-line at the same time to read your headlines.

- Automate your tweets.

What else can you do?

Build a massive Twitter Platform that will help you reach a larger audience.

If you want to learn more, go here:

getBook.at/HTG100K

Comments: Once you learn how to write short and snappy content, that's fun and entertaining, you'll be the talk of the town.

Golden Nugget #33

Why That Title?

Reading Time: 3min 10sec

Jennifer: People have been curious about the title, asking why is it called: Write Like You're Already Famous.

M LeMont: Well, let's talk about it because that's the heart and soul of this book.

Jennifer: The title may appear to be like a contradiction to what we say about "getting your shadow out the way" when writing & marketing.

M LeMont: True, but as we both live & breathe it in our partnership–some contradictions can bring clarity! In this case– it's transparency to the Keys of Writing Success!

Jennifer: Well said LeMont, but let's just put some "Wordsmithing" skills to the test on the word "FAMOUS" since that's what draws attention.

Here are some other words:

- Distinction of Dreams
- Esteemed Respected
- Expertise Prominent

M LeMont: Jen, those are some good words–the title describes a MINDSET. If you Write To Be Famous then you'll be writing like everyone else and playing it safe.

But if you Write Like You're Already Famous–you've given yourself permission to THINK DIFFFERENT and break the rules for a favorable position–an unfair advantage.

It all COMES DOWN TO YOU.

How do you THINK?

Imagine what you could accomplish if you weren't trying to be politically correct and if you removed the shackles of 'proper' or what you think your best English teacher told you was the right way.

Get out your comfort zone.

Think Different.

Standout.

What do you have to lose?

Jennifer: ¡Exactamente! (exactly!) You have Nothing to Lose and Everything to Gain. Thinking differently sets you apart from the crowd. That's Unconventional Inspiration!

Okay, let's go–the jet is waiting to take us to our next writing destination!

Comments: Take your time when choosing a title–it's a critical part of the buying process. You should never create a book cover yourself unless you're a professional designer.

Golden Nuggets #34

Tell Me A Secret...not any ole secret

Reading Time: 2min 2sec

I want to learn all about you...so tell me a Secret.

In the meantime, while you're searching that Beautiful & Mysterious mind of yours...

Let Me Tell You a Secret About Writing.

"Every Life needs another Life.

Every Heart needs another Heart.

Every day is a new day and this just might be your day." ~Kem

Draw Close So You Can Hear Me.

When you're writing, you must make it sound like music–harmonizing ecstasy with every single word into a rhythm, beat, tone and flow.

It makes the STORY come alive with passion and makes the reader read with emotion.

C'MON... I know what I'm talking about.... Passion Will Make You Fall For What You Feel.

Now What's Your Secret?

I told you I want to know all about you, and that's what you should want to know about your readers.

You want to know all about them.

LEARN more writing secrets....

Maybe just for tonight.

Comments: Break the pattern. Pages and pages of narration, setup, background and description can slow the pace and turn your story into a graduation speech.

Golden Nugget #35

Laying Down the Tracks Every Day

Reading Time: 2 min 2 sec

"Write without pay until somebody offers to pay."~Mark Twain

So you want to be a writer, do you? Hell, that may be asking for too much. From the time, you wake in the morning, before the sun starts to rise–when you open your eyes, you have to be selfish with your time–I mean selfish, until the end of time. FOREVER.

You must write every day. That's what real writers do, they write.

LAY Down the Tracks and write 100 words every day. Build the infrastructure that will make you far superior than the rest of the crowd.

Yea. Yea. Yea.

I know I hear the tears rolling down your face. That's too hard!

Well, it will be hard at first, and then it will get easy, and you'll be able to write about anything and you'll be able to do it fast.

I PROMISE.

Practice writing short and snappy sentences that captivate. NO MORE playing it safe– hiding behind intellectually wordy prose that bore the heck out of readers.

I'm SCREAMING at the top of my lungs, and I hear your heart beating like a drum.

I'm TRYING to tell you something–

I write every day, and I can say more in 200 words than what others write in 5,000 words.

Less words mean your readers will get twice as much.

Comments: Read lots of books, listen to music and watch movies–study and analyze techniques, words and phrases. This is how you become better than the rest.

Golden Nugget #36

A Search For Freedom Can Take You Anywhere, Don't Get Drunk on a Dream

Reading Time: 2 min 9sec

"I'm under the impression that a lot of people are now looking at self-publishing as a Get Rich Quick scheme, and there is no such thing. Look what Amanda Hocking accomplished in a year, when they really should be saying–Look what Amanda Hocking accomplished in twenty years. Because that's how long I've been writing, that's how long I've been working towards this goal."

Those are the words of Amanda Hocking who sold over one million books in less than a year in 2010.

Now everyone wants to be the next overnight success story. But that was then and this is now.

Currently, ebooks are surpassing print book consumption and growing at a faster rate. There are over 800 e-books published every day giving readers plenty of choices.

Success is–now you see it, and now you don't.

"Every industry has the pie in the sky, hit the lottery, get rich overnight hopes and dreams."

If you really knew how much authors earn, you'd be shocked. It's a shame that we can't get accurate information about what authors realistically earn.

Amazon and other publishing companies do not disclose author earnings or book sales. So it's hard for new authors to manage their expectations and set realistic goals.

Listen to this.

What you see is an illusion.

When you see a book listed as a Best Seller, you think the book is selling like gangbusters. But what it really means is–Best Seller in it's Genre or Category, which doesn't necessarily equate to a lot of sales.

One sale a day in a weak category could earn an author the Best Seller title, but clearly the author didn't earn very much.

Now that's the biggest illusion of them all. Since publishing companies don't disclose authors' earning, it's hard to find figures unless you get them directly from the authors themselves.

Here are three blogs where authors are straightforward about how much they're earning: Google Search: Amanda Hocking–Epic Tale of How It All Happened, Rachel Thompson–How Much An Author Can Realistically Expect To Make, Part One and Part Two, and Hugh Howey

7K blog. http://authorearnings.com/report/the-report/

So my sweet dumpling, it all boils down to this: A Search for Freedom Can Take You Anywhere; Don't Get Drunk On A Dream. Write because you love it and be so damn good, one day people want to pay you for it.

Golden Nugget #37

The 3 Most Dangerous Thoughts to your Writing Career

Reading Time: 2min 40sec

After publishing my first book, I began to wonder if being an author was really worth it–then I found this quote that changed my perspective.

"...good and bad things would happen to me, but, in the long run, all of it would be converted into words." -Jorge Luis Borges

Wow! How profound is that? It changed my way of thinking, entirely. I began to look at writing in a totally different way.

Life is nothing more than one long Hollywood movie, and as a writer you can carve out a small piece and write about it.

Write because you love it, and manage your expectations.

The reward is in the writing itself.

You have the ability to write it down on paper and bring the story to life. How many people in the world can do that? If you see things differently–then YOU can be different.

The 3 Most Dangerous Thoughts to your writing career

1. You think–you will get famous overnight. The odds are about the same as an athlete getting drafted into the NBA or NFL, a singer becoming a rock star or a person hitting the lottery. This sort of thinking will take the wind out of your sails fast.
2. You think–you will get support from your spouse- Don't count it! And if you get it–good for you. Count your blessings! It's the deadliest threat of the three that can make you quit writing.
3. You think–friends and family will buy your book and give you good reviews. I'm sorry to burst your bubble, but if you think you'll get their support–you're dead wrong. Most friends and family don't care–the only thing they want to know is–how many books have you sold. So don't take it personally, it's just the way it is.

In the meantime, if you write because you love it and manage expectations, "One day, you may be so damn good, they can't ignore you." ~Steve Martin (altered)

Ralph Waldo Emerson said, "Build a better mouse trap than your neighbor and the world will make a beaten path to your door."

(It will be just a matter of time.)

Results live in the future–you have no control over the time or the place.

Golden Nugget #38

Writing Must Become a Habit

Reading Time: 2min 2sec

"Don't quit It's very easy to quit during the first ten years." ~Andre Dubus

Wow! Is that not, a true statement? Everybody wants instant success, but nobody wants to log in the time to be great.

Writers write, that's what they do; not for the money, they write because it's in their blood.

And if you're not striving to be the very best then you should quit now and do something else. You'll never learn your craft well enough to compete and make a living.

LET ME BREAK IT DOWN

If you want to be a real writer, then you must write 100 words every day. Writing must be a HABIT. It must become as routine as putting on your shoes.

Do you have shoes on now?

Do you remember putting them on? PROBABLY NOT. That's how your writing should become–

effortless. And it will get easy if you write 100 words every day.

I write so much that I've forgotten what I've written. If it weren't for my co-author, Jennifer who digs deep into the archives, some of these golden nuggets would be hidden forever.

Anyway, I have a new book that will help you develop the right mindset and become a real writer. Coming soon: Write Like You're Already Famous. And if you're reading the book as we speak–you're already ahead of the game. Bravo!

In the meantime, practice writing 100 words every day. If you have a blog then write a post every day or send a 200 word email to your list.

EVERYDAY–you must write and don't fool yourself... it's going to be hard at first but then it gets easy.

It took me 20 minutes to write this 200 word nugget. It used to take me 4 hours. More importantly, WRITING must become a habit if you want to be a real writer. It will separate you from the crowd because they're not going to do it.

Okay, I have to go and write another Golden Nugget.

Cheers!

Comments: Write for a specific audience– always cite a problem and give a solution.

Golden Nugget #39

Writing for Impact–Profanity or Not?

Reading Time: 2min 20sec

After putting a rear-naked choke on Conor McGregor that ended the fight, during the UFC 196 Main event, Nate Diaz walked over to the sports reporter with a blood soaked face that only Rocky Balboa could appreciate.

"That was some fight. How do you feel?"

"Well, first I want to thank my fans for supporting me. I had only two weeks to train for this fight so I got my ASS kicked for two rounds until I could find my bearings."

"I Also Want To Let Everyone Know That There's a New Mutha....Sheriff In Town!"

LMAO!!!! No bleeps or beeps from the Paid Per View Networks.

Why?

Do you want me to punch you in the nose for asking me something like that? Okay, I'm just kidding.

Anyway, the networks allowed the profanity because it was funny and entertaining.

Should you use profanity when you write? You bet, if it can make a scene Memorable, Laughable, Shocking, or even get you Thinking Differently!

WHAT READERS LIKE IS TO BE ENTERTAINED so give them what they want.

In her book Year of YES, Shonda Rhimes explains that she's an introvert. She describes how it felt for her to write a book about herself:

"Standing on a table in a very proper restaurant, raising my dress and showing everyone that I'm not wearing panties. That is to say, it feels shocking."

Well, guess what? That was shocking–but I take my hat off to her because Shonda gets it. She KNOWS how to shock and entertain an audience.

Bottom line?

Add a little SPICE to your writing and keep your readers guessing what you're going to say next.

Comments: Practice, Practice, Practice– learn how to put a bit of magic into your writing style. Make your words and phrases sing.

Golden Nugget #40

Spanish Dialogue Techniques

Reading Time: 5min 2sec

One of the best ways to learn how to use a foreign language in your novels is to study the techniques of other writers and authors like John Locke.

I try to include a bit of Spanish in my books every chance I get, liven up things up– it's like adding a Chipotle pepper to your writing.

Jennifer: The perfect pinch of that special "spice" makes it –Sabroso–Yummy- Flavorful! When you add a little Spanish language–you're also adding a bit of culture to your book. You give readers a deeper connection to the characters, and bring out the uniqueness of your novel.

Notice how Jen used Spanish and then followed immediately with the English meaning of the word: "Yummy". Never leave it up to the reader to guess what it means–always deliver the Translation quickly.

Jennifer: You don't need to use a lot of Spanish, just a dash to liven things up like we did with Carlos on the airplane and the Chinese waiter in Macao. It gives the reader a fresh reading experience.

I agree. And the language doesn’t have to be used solely as a character's native tongue.

Let me give you an example from one of my novels.

It's about a wife Caught Up in an extramarital affair and a husband who would do anything to save her.

In the scene, the husband confronts his wife's lover on the telephone:

"This is AV Aviation, how can I help you?"

"¿Cuál es su nombre?" What is your name?

"What?? Why?"

"So I can write your name in blood across your forehead. Where I come from, you don't mess with another man's wife."

It didn't matter whether he spoke Spanish or not, I had bad intentions, and anybody who interfered was going down with him. Little did he know–I was sitting outside his office with my finger on the trigger. He was a half a mile from hell.

Jennifer: Oh, I remember that opening scene, neither one of the characters spoke Spanish–how creative.

That's correct, using Spanish in your books allows you to be creative and find ways to intrigue your readers.

Jennifer: How do you decide which words to use, because some Spanish words have different meanings than their English translations?

Well, it's always wise to consult someone that speaks fluent Spanish.

Jennifer: I agree but I know some authors think using Google Translate is the way to go.

The BIG problem with auto translators is–they can give you the wrong word or words with an entirely different meaning that can be rather embarrassing.

So when looking for a Spanish expert–you want someone who speaks Fluent Spanish and has an understanding of the culture and dialect so you know the right words to use.

With this book I got lucky and found Jennifer who speaks and writes in fluent Spanish and is very creative.

Jennifer: Awe, that's nice. It's a lot of fun creating the right things to say in Spanish and finding the perfect 'word recipe'.

So, here's the bottom line–spruce up your writing and add a bit of **'la lengua española'** Spanish language to your work–Think Differently and leave the competition standing in the dust.

And if you need help finding the right words for writing some lines or scene in Spanish, contact Jennifer. Go here: Click

¡Aclamaciones! Cheers!

Golden Nugget #41

What Your Brain Thinks of Self-Editing

Reading Time: 3min 40sec

Okay, Mr. Big Shot, so you want to go against the grain and self-edit your book?

You say you graduated at the top of your class and have a keen eye for catching mistakes.

You were the State Spelling Champion in high school?

Hmm...I don't think your brain cares.

When it comes to editing your own work–your brain doesn't care about your keen eye or academic accomplishments.

If you wrote it and read it many times, your brain knows how it should read and it will trick you into thinking that a word is there when it's really missing–Or that a word is spelled correctly when it's not. You'll be reading–but not really reading.

Do you hear me?

There's some psychological phenomena called Pareidolia–it makes you see things that aren't there–like seeing faces in clouds, images in mountains or a river in the desert.

Your brain knows what you intended to say, it knows what you think you wrote–so it makes you see exactly that.

Anyway, if you insist on going against the grain, here are 9 helpful tips:

1. Just before your final read through, get away from your novel for 60-90 days. When you read it again, you'll have fresh eyes and will see things differently.

2. Read your entire manuscript out loud. You'll recognize when it sounds stifled or the flow is interrupted with mistakes and excess words.

3. You can use a Text-to-Voice Software program to read your manuscript out loud.

4. Keep a list of words that you commonly make mistakes on:

Your/you're, were/where/we're, that/which To/Too

There/their/they're, fill/feel, now/know, new/knew, form/from, who/how, etc.

Then use the Find feature on Windows and locate those words.

5. Change the font or word size of your text to something different than the original–like Times Romans to Garamond.

6. Read your book on a different device. This will trick your brain into believing the content is brand new.

7. Publish your book a few days before the official release date. Buy the book and read it on a mobile device–highlight mistakes, correct and upload changes.

8. Don't rely on Microsoft Spell Check to catch grammar, or past and present tense mistakes.

A low cost alternative, is Grammarly.com 80%-90% accuracy.

Well, there you go my esteemed Governor–I sure hope that information helps. Just remember, there's no substitute for the advice of a welltrained professional–Proofreader, Editor or Wordsmith.

Golden Nugget #42

When Bad Things Happen

Reading Time: 2min 35sec

When I took a load of clothes out the dryer, my clothes were ruined with ink stains. The dryer drum had ink everywhere. Apparently, a pen exploded. Now I was looking at buying another dryer. (Estimated cost $500.)

So I worked feverously to remove the ink. I tried everything from Windex to nail polish remover, and nothing worked.

Do you hear me? NOTHING. But there was a ray of hope as the thought came...

What could I find on Google?

Take three towels soak them in a bucket of bleach and then squeeze them dry. Place towels inside the dryer. Turn the dryer on for a full cycle. Whooooo! It worked.

And it also gave meaning to the quote:

"Nothing bad ever happens to a writer."

Why? Because a writer can write about anything that happens to him.

People love to hear stories, especially when it relates to a problem and a solution.

So, incorporate stories into your writings and keep the reader interested. We all have common problems.

The same is true about using Twitter. The problem is most people are stuck, at 200 followers and can't find a solution.

Take this email I received:

"I have a high regard for this woman b/c she shares wonderful educational posts that do so much to help people. I retweet her posts all the time and never once has she ever retweeted for me."

Well, that's the problem in a nutshell.

You had a high regard for the woman, and she didn't have the same regard for you.

I want you to do something for me.

Well actually, two things.

Can you do them?

I know you don't know what they are.

Commit first and I'll tell you.

Okay!

First–never be impressed with someone's seemingly good actions or accomplishments! It's nothing but bullshit anyway. If you strip them of the non-essentials, you'll see what they're made of. Then you can be impressed.

NOW come closer so you can hear me clearly.

Stop worrying what people think about you. Imagine what you could accomplish if you didn't worry about fear of rejection or criticism?

That's FREEDOM very few people will ever experience.

Y OTRA COSA, (another thing)... if you want to reverse the situation and have people impressed with you–make your Twitter account valuable like a piece of real estate in the sky.

I guarantee that woman would have seen you differently if you had 100,000+ followers. Yes, I know, stupid! But unfortunately that's how people think.

Anyway, on the business side if you want to learn how to play the game, go here: getBook.at/HTG100K

Golden Nugget #43

Get Behind The Mule

Reading Time: 3min 31sec

My wife told me I worked too much, and she didn't marry a man, she married a mule. So I told her:

"You've got to get behind the mule. Plow!

~Tom Waits

Are you a good Storyteller?

Good stories can hook the reader into reading more.

I got a letter from a 9-year old kid that lived in Michigan. He said, "I brought one of your records to school, and I got in a lot of trouble. Now I have to go to court. Can you help?"

I said, "Listen I got things... I got things to do. I mean, I have a life.

You may not think so, but I've got a life."

"I'm glad you bought my records, but I'VE got plenty of SHIT to do.

I know you may not think I have anything else to do, but I can't just drop everything, jump on a plane, and fly my ASS to Michigan and represent you in court.

What kind of guy do you think I am?

I just make records for GOODNESS SAKE."

******

Hilarious! Well, I thought so anyway.

Now Tom Waits, the famous songwriter could take a simple story like that and give it a beat and sell a million records. (story altered)

To become a good storyteller, you must study the works of top storytellers: songwriters, copywriters, movie writers, singers, authors, and actors.

People love to hear stories.

Write simple stories with HOOKS in your NARRATIVE and an OPENING that locks the reader into your book.

Bend your ears and listen to the rhythm and the heartbeat...

Short.

Snappy.

Words and phrases.

"You've got to get behind the mule. Plow!"

Never let the weeds get too high–long narratives and set up bogs down your story.

Comments: Did you notice the Hook? "You've got to get behind the mule. Plow!" The common mistake most writers make–they are too wordy. Superfluously wordy to the 3rd degree. Tons and tons of wasted words. Get rid of the excess–make your writing crisp and tight. Plow! Write short. Stand out.

Golden Nugget #44

Down the Rabbit Hole

Reading Time: 2min 12sec

"When I write, I slip into a dream state although my eyes are wide open. Then I see how deep the rabbit hole goes. Sometimes it's shallow and other times I'm 'in there,' writing for hours."

Authors try to force the process and often never finish their work because they didn't Trust the Source, Where All Things Come From.

Are you listening to me?

Yes, there is a Higher Power where ideas come from, as well as your own thoughts.

Sorry, I know you want to be in control and take credit for an idea; but you've never had an original thought in your life. Neither have I. No one has. And if you think that you have, then tell me where you keep your thoughts... in your pocket?

When I write, I never get writer's block. I write everything in my mind. Then, when the ideas come, I rush to catch as many of them as I can before they disappear back to their sacred hiding place.

And, when ideas come it's usually at the most awkward times–when I'm driving, taking a shower, making love, etc. and who knows why.

I just know those ideas don't care if you're ready or not.

Writing is fun if you learn to TRUST THE SOURCE FROM WHERE ALL THINGS COME FROM.

Down the Rabbit Hole–see where it takes you.

Golden Nugget #45

So You Think You Can Captivate Me?

Reading Time: 2min 2sec

You think you can satiate my voracious appetite for reading?

What! You think you got what it takes for me to read YOUR BOOK, all the way to the end?

I get bored quickly! That's why I read three books at the same time.

Okay, let me see what you've got?

Wow, is that it? You can't even get next to me with that. If you don't get me in the first few pages, I'm out...gone!

You see, JACKIE O–you have to do more than just play it safe if you want me to read YOUR BOOK.

Give me something NEW...something FRESH.

You have to dive deep.

Did you get that?

You've gotta go deeper.

Then you might be able to captivate me so I'll read your book to the end.

Call me tomorrow.

Comments: Good writing is the sound and melody of words that break off into a song. I often dance to the rhythm of a great book. Reading books of a different genre while I write is one of my favorite writing techniques.

Golden Nugget #46

Words! Brilliant words and Phrases

Reading Time: 2min 10sec

I recall a story of a woman who found a famous author on the floor holding his head. She asked if he was okay, and he said I'm trying to find the right word for this sentence, and he pounded his fists on the floor and screamed I've been down here for hours, and I can't find it!

I spend hours arranging and rearranging words, for tweets, captions, headlines that evoke emotions. I am an artist–a painter and so are you whether you know it or not. You tweet, don't you?

I paint every day, not with a brush and canvas, but with words. Brilliant words and phrases that make people feel good. If I were painting you, then you would be my Mona.... Lisa.

When words are properly arranged they can create the rhythm and flow of a sentence, paragraph or page.

You can be an awesome writer if you unloosen the shackles of things you've been taught. Are you listening to me? You're walking around with a ball and chain.

And here's something else—Remember?? Ok I'll tell you again because it bares repeating…

Don't worry about fear of rejection or criticism. Just write!

To write is to paint with words. Now, when you find an artist like that, then you've got to keep them. Learn from them–read everything they write.

Comments: Words can slow or speed up the story. To slow the pace–add descriptions, thoughts, quotes and speeches. Or, add more dialogue with powerful verbs and nouns to speed things up. Stay away from a lot of adjectives.

Golden Nugget #47

Geez Your Posts Make me Float Like I'm on Dope. How Can I Write Like That?

Reading Time: 2min 2sec

Well, I sure in hell hope you don't mean that literally because dope isn't good for you. I just want to make that perfectly clear before we go any further.

Now listen carefully, I'm going to tell you a little secret. When I was nine years old, I use to wear suits to school and carry a briefcase.

The other kids would tease and laugh at me. My mother said, "Don't worry son, one day those kids will be working for you. They will be your employees. You keep on being you!"

Now that's the first thing you gotta do–**Be YOU** and not like everyone else.

Do you hear me?

Write, like you're having a conversation with your friends at the kitchen table. All of you are relaxed and having fun, and you're not worried about your grammar or trying to be politically correct. And if you are then that's just plain stupid. 'Find you some new friends!'

And one other thing: practice, practice, practice.

Write 100 words every day in a blog post or email until you find your unique voice. It will be hard at first, but then it will get easier with time.

Now, go forth my esteemed governor, the world awaits you.

Comments: Creative writing is the pleasure of reading the right words, arranged in the right order that inspire and stretch the imagination.

Golden Nugget #48

Make Trolls Your Interns and Keep Moving

Reading Time: 2min 2sec

Buried deep in the jungle of Amazon.com under 90+ Five Star reviews, you'll find–if you scroll down far enough, a lonely, alienated, 1-star review on How To Gain 100,000 Twitter Followers.

When you read, you'll think the person who wrote it is on METH or something. I mean, totally disjointed, ranting about who knows what???

Then, a few days later I received an email that said "Loser!" Obviously, the same troll who gave me the 1-Star.

Now, what is an author to do? Well, you can either ignore it or complain to Amazon. (good luck) I don't run from bullshit like that; I'm a writer.

I write, that's what I do. I write every day, and I write about everything and anything where there's a lesson to be learned.

So, I made this troll my INTERN to bring more attention to my book.

Most interns work without pay; now that seems like a fair exchange. How much is free publicity worth these days?

I'll make a few sales for every ten people that read this post. And guess what? Once I write a post, it resonates on the Internet forever; for the next generation to read.

Anyway, the lesson: don't run, WRITE! Make trolls your interns!

Comments: Writers have the best job on the planet and can create anything with words. Don't ever make a writer mad, you may end up as a character in their book.

Golden Nugget #49

Where Were You?

Reading Time: 2min 20sec

"If winning is a fault, then I plead guilty. I like to win. I don't know any other way–it's in my blood. When I get beaten... & that happens occasionally, I like it to be by an opponent who's worthy of my respect." Bear Bryant, Coach: Birmingham, Alabama

Where were you? When Bear Bryant delivered that speech?

Where were you? when you heard that Dr. Martin Luther King Jr, and John F Kennedy were assassinated?

Let's reflect back.

Where were you?

When racial prejudice RAN rampant in Birmingham, Alabama, and Governor George Wallace said, "I draw a line in the sand, segregation today, segregation tomorrow, and segregation forever."

Tell me, *WHERE WERE YOU?*

When Martin Luther King called, "Birmingham the most thoroughly segregated city in the United States."

Tell me, DO YOU EVER THINK ABOUT...All the killings and bombings?

I remember, and I know where I was.

The emptiness and the spiritual bleakness of those dark days will never be forgotten. And if we're not careful, what lies ahead could be worse than what we experienced in the past.

"If you only love those that love you back, what kind of love is that?"

I'm sitting here writing my next book, and watching the movie Woodlawn, and I was compelled to ask, WHERE WERE YOU?

I know where I was, and I'll never forget.

Comments: Feel good about what you do. As a writer, you have the power of the pen to influence the world–use it.

Golden Nugget #50

What You Should Know First... before you publish.

Reading Time: 2min 2 sec

"There's a good chance only your mother cares you wrote a book. If, knowing this, you can write another one; you're probably a writer." ~@OneWritersTrip

After writing my first book and discovering the "shocking truth" that nobody cared, I summoned the strength to write my next book and then another and yet another until I had written six books in a year.

Jennifer: I think writers are writers even when they are not writing. It's something inside of us that emerges at the right moment. How did you actually get to that place…"The Writing Place?"

Well, most writers are born to write, but I never wanted to be a writer–actually I abhorred the idea. Then one day, I heard about Kindle self-publishing and decided that writing books would be an excellent business to get into. Now I'm obsessed with writing.

Later, I discovered the hard truth: Writing is a lonely game, like living on an island playing solitaire every day. You don't write to get rich.

No sir, you write because you love the game. You love taking something from the invisible and bringing it to the physcial.

Jennifer: Real writers create and evoke emotion with words–they keep writing and they do it for little or no pay. When we write together, I feel like we are painting a picture in the sky with our words...it's ethereal because we both are in sync and we love where the words can take the reader.

That's right honey, and, who knows–when writers feel like that, one day they may be so damn good, people will want to pay to get that book in their hands.

So keep writing. Never give up. Never.

Comments: When you give readers valuable insights and information they look forward to hearing about your products and services. Offer a link to every writing piece. I give plenty of examples on how to make the transition from information to product, so study these Golden Nuggets.

Golden Nuggets #51

Where Do Ideas Come From?

Reading Time: 3min 20 sec

Well, for me it's knowing and trusting THE SOURCE, WHERE ALL THINGS COME FROM.

But it's sort of like trying to explain some paranormal event to someone. So, I want you to stop right now and listen to a Ted Talks video by Elizabeth Gilbert, who describes the process as clear as rain: **Your Elusive Creative Genius.**

Okay, I hear what you're saying..."I'm not going to stop and watch a Freakin' video?"

Now, don't be lazy.

FOR GOODNESS SAKE, this is your writing career we're talking about here.

You bought this book to learn how to THINK, and we're going to use every resource available to teach you–even enlisting the help of experts. But if you still need some convincing, here's some highlights from the TED TALK Video.

Ruth Stone the famous poet said, "When I was growing up as a little girl working in the field, I could hear and feel an idea coming over the landscape. I didn't have a pen and paper, so I had to run like hell to the house before the idea would barrel through me and keep going until it found another poet to penetrate.

Sometimes I would almost miss as it passed through me and I'd catch it by its tail and pull it backwards into my body, and it would come out on the page backwards from the last word to the first."

Then there's a brief story about Tom Waits, the songwriter. He was driving down the freeway and received an idea about a melody.

He had...

No Pen.

No Paper.

No Recorder.

What was he to do?

He looked up at the sky and said, *"Can you not see that I'm driving? Does it look like I can write down a song right now?*

If you want me to have this idea, can you come back later at a more opportune time when I'm better prepared?" Or you can go on down the road and bother someone else."

He trusted The Source, Where All Things Come From and knew another idea would come later that would be even better.

Yes, my dear reader, I think you want to watch this Ted Talks video. Google the title: Your Elusive Creative Genius Elizabeth Gilbert TED Talks.

We'll wait right here.

You can also Google the title: Your Elusive Creative Genius Elizabeth Gilbert TED Talks.

Comments: LeMont, this talk was one of those "IT" moments for us while writing together! We would both agree it taps into those intangible yet palpable moments in a writer's experience when it feels as if you simply "swallow the sun" and the light of inspiration flows through you onto the page.

When we become aware of the constant flow of ideas available and tap into this Great Source–something ethereal occurs that is far above our own human reasoning.

Golden Nugget #52

Firecracker Writing Skills

Reading Time: 2 min 2 sec

The ad read:

" Looking for someone to operate a firecracker stand for two weeks Dec. 20- Jan. 1. "

- No investment.
- Earn 20% of gross; estimated sales $50k.
- 9 am to midnight.
- Cannot leave premises.
- Must sleep in firecracker stand every day for two weeks.
- No water, no heat, no air condition, no breaks.
- Portable toiletry pod on site. "Adventure of a lifetime."

Now, I love to study a well-constructed ad.

I'm going to share what I learned.

Draw close so you won't miss it.

To find his market, the writer purposely accentuated the negative to reject a certain percentage of people who wouldn't work a firecracker stand under such miserable conditions.

He drilled down to find his target audience by using certain words and phrases to IGNITE a PASSION that already existed in the right prospects.

Now tell me, what do you think he was trying do?

When this passion intersected with the "right moment in time," the prospect wise enough to see the benefit would be ready to buy.

When TIME and DESIRE, intersect. Did you get that? It's the essence of marketing your product.

Good writers know how to strike a nerve and use words to build value and tap a desire that already exists at a special moment in time.

To become a great writer, you must learn the craft.

Comments: Are you writing with too many words to describe a person, place, or thing? Cut the excess and add flavor to the story. Less is more and more words mean less enjoyment for the reader.

Golden Nugget #53

Do you know the difference between a Proofreader, Editor, and Wordsmith?

Reading time: 3 min 2 sec

Words…the most inexhaustible source of magic we have. And though many work with words, there is ONE who's different than the rest! The **WORDSMITH**.

But first let me introduce TWO others who also play an important role in your writing success.

Hello there **Proofreader!** You have a perfectionist's eye for catching mistakes. You are a natural nick-picker by heart–and writers wouldn't have it any other way!

We owe you a debt of gratitude for those eyes of yours! Oh–those EYES so keenly focused. It's like someone noticing a tiny snag on MY pantyhose. OH! Thank you, Proofreaders, for catching those snags before they run wild and ruin THINGS.

I mean look at all you do for us as writers– fixing our spelling, grammar, punctuation errors, typos, missing or duplicated words, inconsistency of verb tenses and a multitude of other grammar issues.

Plus, I wish every proofreader was as good as you, but as you know there are good ones and–bad ones, and Oh My GOD–a bunch of "FAKE" ones that take your money and run.

Okay, Next up: meet the **Editors**.

We writers could not do without you even for a minute, although most are confused at what you really do.

You see, many writers think you're–a proofreader but you have your own special talent.

You are like a hostile takeover–RUTHLESS, BOLD, BRAZEN, and HEARTLESS–revising scenes and wiping out entire chapters.

To an author, YOU are the most abhorred person on planet earth.

I mean, where do you get the nerve to tell me, my opening narrative is long and boring when my friends and family liked it?

Then you tell me to revise a scene that I was so passionate about.

How dare you!

You completely DISRUPT things– dialogues, narrative, move chapters around; or anything else you boldly decide MUST be done to improve the book.

Listen!

I told you I love it and I do! I need you Mr. Editor. I need you on my team. Thank you for helping me see the light.

Okay, finally I must introduce you to the last of the trio: The **WordSmith**, who you probably don't know anything about.

The WORDSMITH is a Curator of Words. who uses the right words to make a story so INTENSE, so INTIMATE that it evokes PASSION in the hearts of your readers.

• The WORDSMITH AROUSES the mind effortlessly stringing words together and conjuring up an array of muti-hued EMOTIONS.

• The Wordsmith arranges and weaves words into sentences and phrases improving the sound, rhythm and flow of the writing.

• One word can make a whole page BRILLIANT!

Radiant and elegant words can make your book a page turner...the reader has no time to yawn or take a nap.

M LeMont once told someone, "Forget about proofreading, forget about editing, I can find people to do that stuff for a dime a dozen. But finding a WORDSMITH, now that's something special."

So friends keep your eyes open and you'll know when you find one because their words will excite you.

Comments: Jennifer, thanks so much for THAT forensic explanation. Good advice.

One other thing, don't ever try and Proofread, Edit, or Wordsmith your own book because your brain will trick you into seeing things that aren't there. Let the natural instincts of a Wordsmith like Jen illuminate your page. Also, if you need some ideas about adding Spanish to your writing, go here: thejennieration.com

Golden Nugget #54

What Are You Willing to Give Up?

Reading time: 9min 24sec

Take No days off>>Don't eat>>Don't Sleep>>Let them Eat>>Let them Sleep. Work Harder>>Work Smarter than everybody else..

Brilliant! Genius! Magnificent!

That's what I've been called, but it's not true. It only appears that way because I did something that most people wouldn't dare do.

I showed up and went to work when everyone was asleep.

Showing up is 90% of the battle and you'll look to others like you've climbed Mt Everest.

I wake up and go to work. I'm a writer, so I write every day.

It doesn't matter what I write about as long as I write something every day.

That's why I'm writing to you right now.

I'd rather work 80 hours a week for myself, so I won't have to work 40 hours a week for "The Man".

But most people don't see it that way, they think work is work and you leave it at the door after you've put in your time.

Some folks are inherently lazy, slothful, and too busy with things that don't contribute anything to their success.

Jennifer: What is the key that opens the door to success? What is it that will help people to work smarter, because setting aside your life, putting in that many hours, not eating, not sleeping...that's not success to me.

Well, Jen success is something everyone has to determine for themselves. How badly do you want it and what are you willing to give up to get it?

What I want to do here is move people to action and let everyone know that if you want to succeed then you have to be willing to make sacrifices and for some it may not be worth it.

In a perfect world, you look for BALANCE, but in the early stages and in a world with Mega Competition there is no such thing as BALANCE.

You must work your ass off–reach down and push your mind and body until it cries for mercy.

I'm reminded, of a quote from the movie "Miracle" where the coach told his hockey team, when facing up against a formidable opponent–

"This Can Not Be A Team of Common Men Because Common Men Go Nowhere–To Win You Must Be Uncommon."

Success requires doing things nobody else wants to do and that means: HARD WORK, SACRIFICES, and WORKING SMART.

You do have three good points there! Working Hard is a lot more effective when it's combined with working Smart. And, any kind of success requires an amount of sacrifice.

Yes, but Hard Work by itself is not going to get it. I can get a donkey to work hard, but I can't get him to WORK SMART–to find the right tools, strategies, and people to connect with.

I LOVE the quote you shared because it's an example of Marketing w Meaning! Building a Twitter Tribe of 'Common Men' would be easy...but creating a team of uncommon unconventional thinkers–ready to explore what is "outside the norm"–now that's where working smart comes into play!

That's for damn sure, you are catching on and you know how to catch the big fish don't you!

Jennifer: Hey, what happened to the "ego aside" thing?? Hahajahaja! Ok, yes– you big fish you!

Anyway, if I didn't scare the crap, out of everybody, then How To Gain 100,000 Twitter Followers is a good place to start. Work smart and use the right tools & strategies to find the right people to connect with.

Your numbers will soar. I guarantee it! Here's the link: getBook.at/HTG100K

And, if you don't have a Kindle, download the free app for PC, Cell, and Tablet.

Comments: This was a hard-hitting motivational post that got a lot of attention. It separates the doers from the fakes. Don't be afraid to tell it like it is–Raw honesty–most people will appreciate and can't wait to learn more by clicking your link. Now study the headline for effect–use short and snappy nouns and verbs–stay away from adjectives.

Now you know what I'm about to say here–

Take No days off>>Don't eat>>Don't Sleep>>Let them Eat>>Let them Sleep. Work Harder>>Work Smarter than everybody else.

Golden Nugget #55

Can Words Be Hot...Or Just Women?

Reading Time: 2min 2sec

I remember the day as clear as rain. "She's not the only one you know. Since you don't want to collaborate, maybe you need two Wordsmiths. I'm pretty good. You'll see."

The more we messaged each other, the more her words tantalized and captivated me. Her words were HOT–Intellectually Witty & Snappy.

I was hooked. She had me falling for her... falling with her, falling to her, falling after her, and falling over her. Sometimes PASSION will make you fall for what you feel.

Beautiful ones always SMASH the picture.~Prince

But, not this time.

So Can Words BE Hot...Or Just Women?

Words!! Brilliant Words!! Can take readers to places they've never been before.

Sometimes I have to pinch myself to be sure that readers are talking about a book that I wrote. Then I realized that it wasn't me who deserved the credit. It was my WORDSMITHS that made the books shine!

"Thoroughly enjoyed your HTG100K book. Got lots of revelations. What is most important is your unique voice that differentiates your book from the rest."

Shh! Kiss Me Baby, "An ode to the Master planner and his great design, it's as bare & intense as the adventure it chronicles. The author's unique style of writing interchanging 3 narratives fluidly and masterfully makes it a memorable read."

Now if you want to take your writing to a HIGHER level send me a message and I'll give you the email addresses of my two Wordsmiths.

Remember this is private between you and I. And if you go around bragging about it, then I will have to hunt you down...

Are we clear?

No...No I'm just joking! I had you going there for a minute didn't I? Alright, I was just kidding, here's my email. bob@mistersalesman.com Now get your groove on and get a good Wordsmith. Cheers!

Comments: When writing don't be afraid to push the boundaries, and provide a literary shock that keeps your readers engaged and wondering what's going to happen next.

Golden Nugget #56

Where Did You Get Those Skills?

Reading time: 2min 10sec

"I like your daily posts because they are short, snappy, and filled with valuable information. Is that a skill anybody can learn?"

Thank you for the compliment. The answer is **YES**, it is a skill that anybody can learn, but it takes writing 100 words every day–posts or emails. My posts are roughly 200-300 words.

The average person reads about 150 words a minute. So it takes maximum time 2 min and 2 seconds to read.

I stole that line from Chuck Woolery of the Love Connection. When it was time for a commercial break, Chuck would say, "We'll be back in 2 min and 2 seconds."

Today, with everyone's attention span so short, most people never finish an article anyway. They scan to find the meat as fast as they can. But when you read my posts there's no scanning allowed. I don't care if you don't like it as long as you finish reading it.

I can say as much in 250 words as most writers say in 5,000.

Believe it or not, readers get twice as much when you say less.

If you want to learn how to write short and snappy, then study the works of other writers, and practice.

Comments: Writing a blog post is no different than writing a chapter in a book. Be careful with long– boring expositions, setup, and description at the beginning of your story–come out with guns blazing, and explain later. Sprinkle back in some information through action and dialogue.

Golden Nugget #57

What A Wonderful World

Reading Time: 2min 17sec

"I don't know much about history; I don't know much about biology, I don't know much about Science books; And I don't know much about the French I took; but I do know that I love you, and I know if you love me too what a wonderful this world be." ~Sam Cooke

That song hit the top of charts back in 1960. Then sixteen years after Sam's death in 1987, it was used in the film: What A Wonderful World.

So what's the reason for the success of this seemingly silly song? Well, I'm glad you asked.

It was the use of short and snappy words and sentences seamlessly connected that made a sticky impression in your mind. It didn't matter whether it all made sense or not; it was the hook, rhythm, and flow that made the song so popular.

Now don't speak–just listen, Shhhhhhhh!

Here's a valuable lesson:

If you want to write a book that readers will pick up and read to the end, then write for effect and not to impress.

ELIMINATE long boring narrations, setup, filler words, and descriptive phrases. It's not about word count! Remember: it's about hooks, rhythm, and flow.

Give the reader a memorable experience and they will tell everyone about it.

My latest work: getBook.at/HTG100K

Comments: It's best to read your writing out loud and see if it has good rhythm and tone. If it doesn't sound like music but sounds stifled or has dead spots, then cut and rewrite.

Golden Nugget #58

EPIC2316

Reading time: 1min 54sec

"Have we not each experienced the sensation that a beautiful moment seemed to pass too quickly and wished that we could make it linger?"~The Illunionist

What is your way of remembering something so fantastic that it takes your breath away?

When you close your eyes, do you let your MIND wander over hills and mountains and galaxies to find that BEAUTIFUL moment in time.

Or do you fly in a big yellow balloon begging your thoughts to show you the way?

I don't' care if you have to cross the DESERT in a boat, you find that BEAUTIFUL MOMENT AND HOLD ON TO IT FOREVER.

It will lift your spirits when you are down.

I had one of those BEAUTIFUL MOMENTS. I WISHED I COULD MAKE LINGER ~

I gave it a name: EPIC2316 so I would never forget.

Now, what about that necklace or ring you're sporting–step to the left and let the memories linger.

Don't Write To Be Famous, Write Like You're Already Famous.

Golden Nugget #59

Live Wire: I Fly Solo

Reading Time: 3min 10sec

'Collaborations'–Yes, I know, 'Mr. I fly solo!' Listen to me this time, okay? It's not bad for personalities to clash as long as your inner qualities are stronger than your outer personalities.

Did you get that M LeMont?

Yes, this is me, Jennifer Lopez. Your future writing partner... you'll see.

I got it, Jen...I got it. You are definitely my LIVE WIRE and you take me HIGHER and HIGHER. It's crazy how you already know 'I'm upside down!' But with you I don't have to be right side round.' You know we can't 'find paradise on the ground.' ~Oh Wonder

See, we even like the same music... You know you are a beautiful mess of contradictions, just like me! So, wrap your head around it!

Bring it all to the party, and leave it right there on the table ~ do it with me!

Now TOGETHER we can find a way to create something great! We could be like two singers who come together and write a beautiful melody and sing the duet to the world.

Okay I've given it a lot of thought and have something in mind.

It's true, a major mistake in our industry is the fact that authors simply don't work on enough projects together. I almost made the same mistake if my 'Unreasonable Coach' Buzzmaster, hadn't kicked me in the ass.

Really? What coach?

Didn't you know that I had a coach?

You never told me... and being that you've always said, "I fly solo.." Well, I didn't give it a second thought.

M LeMont: You thought I came up with all my brilliant ideas, entirely on my own?

Well, I'm not that smart, but you know I'm not that dumb either.

Here's what My 'Unreasonable Coach' said, "So what if your personalities clash and you write differently? Put your heart in her hands and her heart in yours–feel the passion, two writers can have when they create something remarkable."

How I could I resist?

Jennifer: You're lucky to have this guy watchin' out for you!

When it comes to writing books two heads could be better than one. EXPLORE the possibilities.

¡Que dulce es! How SWEET it is when two authors work to put aside egos, pride, personalities and self-will, in order to find that sweet spot of inspiration. It's like SUGAR to my SOUL.

Thanks, Jen for your unyielding persistence–I couldn't have written this book without you.

Comments: We all know that 1+1 equal 2. But in the realm of Collaboration 1+1=3, because of the endless supply of ideas that flow from, through, and around each collaborator. Two heads are really better than one. The benefit outweighs the difficulty by a wide margin.

Section 4: The Whole Purpose of Marketing

The Whole Purpose of Marketing is to find ways to STAND OUT and get NOTICED.

ONE Rule, "Move fast and break things."

THE FOUR R's of Book MARKETING

Book Marketing is about getting the **RIGHT** book, cover, and title in front of the **RIGHT** person at the **RIGHT** time and with the **RIGHT** advertising copy that evokes emotions. That takes operating on multiple channels and using MARKETING strategies consistently that work.

Golden Nugget #60

Do You Know The Story of Earnest Shackleton?

Reading Time: 2min 2sec

NOTICE:

Men Wanted For Hazardous Journey–

SMALL WAGES. BITTER COLD.

Long Months of Complete, Darkness.

Constant Danger. Safe Return, Doubtful.

Honor & Recognition in case of success.~

The acclaimed advertisement depicts how Ernest Shackleton recruited the right men for an epic polar expedition of a lifetime.

Twenty-eight men to be exact, all made history. After a long and treacherous–icy voyage–they all made it back home alive.

The men were courageous, brave, daring, adventurous, and willing to sacrifice, to accomplish their ultimate goal...an endurance Expedition to ANTARCTICA.

So I decided to create a similar ad and see how many writers would apply for the position.

There's a market for every product and service–it's just a matter of finding it–time, patience, and method required.

The Emerald Project

WRITERS WANTED

MEN AND WOMEN

For An Uncertain Journey

Little Pay In the Beginning

Years of Hard work

Dedication. Sacrifice. Isolation.

Must be ready to accept criticism from family and friends.

If project is completed successfully–

RECOGNITION

FREEDOM to spend your life as you want

NO BOSS

POT of GOLD at the end

NO GUARANTEES, NO GUARANTEES

Applicants Apply @Mistersalesman

Now that's the life of a writer, but who thinks of it that way when you're aspiring to be one?

Most authors write their first book, and never write another one because they thought it was going to be easy.

It's best before you embark on a new journey, to dig two graves.

One grave is for the way you used to think because the new journey demands that you Think Differently, and the other for all the criticism you must endure.

Then you might begin to dig for what's important: a deeper hole to create your well. Now fill it daily with fresh thoughts and look into that well to draw your inspiration. Learn all you can, pour in fresh ideas daily, and do what it takes to make it happen, instead of looking for overnight success.

Anything worth having–is worth working for, so expect it to be hard–really hard. In the end, it will be worth it.

Anyway, if you need help navigating the stormy seas and growing your Twitter account then grab a copy of my best selling book HTG100K–go here:

getBook.at/HTG100K

Comments: Okay, let's dive right in. Just like Ernest Shackleton *found 28 men–all you need is to find 1,000 customers who like to read your books, who will tell their friends and can't wait to buy your next one. The marketing piece drills down to find the right prospects–who are ambitious and willing to sacrifice to get what they want. It arouses curiosity and transitions into a call to action.*

I took a story that already existed and made it different–better for a new purpose. Now re-read the ad and study the arrangement of words, the sentence structure, tone, and pace.

This marketing piece runs every day on Twitter, and the headline reads: Do you know the Story of Earnest Shackleton? getBook.at/HTG100K #Writers #Authors #Marketing #SMM

Now let me ask you something before we continue.

Are you offended because I included my book link at the end the Golden Nugget? If so, why? How else are you going to learn how to promote, write, and sell your products?

Throughout these pages, I dispense valuable information with a call to action. And if you don't include a link to your product in your writings–tweets, blog posts, or email lists then you're doing yourself and your readers a great disservice.

Some of you may think it's too self-promotional–I guess you could end your writings with a lot more free stuff that you offer, no link, and apologize for having a thumbnail of your book pinned somewhere on your page.

Don't make prospects work to find your link–make it easy for them to buy–they have other things to do.

You should never feel guilty for providing links to your product when 95% of your writing is useful information. Plus, it's how you pay the bills.

Alright, now that I have that out the way, let's keep moving because I have a lot more to teach you.

Golden Nugget #61

The High Cost of Chasing Cheap

Reading Time: 2min 2 sec

The High Cost of Chasing Cheap information is you will always get inferior and low-quality knowledge.

Free information is everywhere–Google it or download a free book.

Recently, I received this message:

"Ok so what's the cost?"

Whenever I get a message like that, it means one thing.

Price Shopper–wants something for NOTHING.

I replied: You tell me, how much would you pay for information that would give you an enormous advantage over the competition?

"Nothing lol! I would give it as a gift to help others. Can you gift it for me?"

Now if that had been 20 years ago, I would have told you, BRACE yourself because I'm about to say something RUDE.

But instead, I CHILLED. I didn't respond.

He was Chasing Cheap.

The lesson?

YOU GET WHAT YOU PAY FOR.

Low price means Low Quality.

And in the end,

The Rich Get Richer, and The Poor Get Poorer

Anyway, if you're interested in how to increase your Twitter followers to get an Unfair Advantage over the competition, go here: But I warn you, cheap is not in the description.

getBook.at/HTG100K

Comments: That's a marketing piece written to attract prospects who are looking for high quality content and willing to pay the price. It's also designed to repel the low price shopper. Notice the attention grabbing headline and hashtags: The High Price of Chasing Cheap is Hurting Price

Shoppers. getBook.at/HTG100K #SMM #SocialMedia #Marketing

Golden Nugget #62

People Have Gone Ape Shit, Thanking People Way Too Much

Reading Time: 2min 20 sec

"I have to say, the level of public thanking has been raised excessively in the USA. We do things differently, says an English friend." ~Tudor

It has become an epidemic on Twitter–thanking people for following and retweets.

There is a gross misunderstanding that thanking someone is appropriate Twitter etiquette. Even Twitter banned automated follow backs; that should have been a hint, right there.

Sending a thank you without giving that person a PROPER RETWEET of something meaningful to them, is flat out disrespectful.

- It shows that you want something for nothing. That's right, you want to be their friend without earning it.
- It means you are too busy to dig deep and find something meaningful to discuss or retweet.

- It takes more than a thank you to win friends and build relationships.
- It also means–when you say, "Thank you for the awesome retweets." What you're really saying is–please keep retweeting my posts, so I can reach a larger audience and I will keep saying thank you.

"User!" Who do you think you are? Other people want to expand their market too!

Okay, you say I'm going a bit overboard?

Maybe, but probably not. Look at some Twitter profiles and you'll see what I mean. Some profiles are filled to the brim with thanking people.

A friend got this tweet from a follower who he thanked a dozen times.

Please, you're killing me–stop thanking me. I get the point.

But the other follower didn't get the point. He was too lazy, or into his on self-promotions, to do anything else, except say thank you to the person every day.

He hoped that was enough to keep the follower retweeting for him.

But, "Thank you" loses its effect after awhile.

The fastest way to win someone's favor is to retweet their book, website, pictures or product.

Then what you're saying is, "Hey, I'm retweeting instead of saying thank you for following me.

I want to get to know you– I'm interested in what you share and perhaps one day, my followers or I will be getting your book or product.

But thanking someone every chance you get is a lazy and selfish man's approach that leads nowhere.

I watch helplessly as hundreds and thousands of "thank you's" stream across my computer screen. Today, I got tired and decided to let everyone know.

It's okay, you're under no obligation–you can stop–you won't wind up in Twitter jail because you don't say, 'Thank You.'

So, please don't expect a thank you from us, it's business–we'll find something meaningful in your profile to retweet.

Hopefully, you have your favorite tweet pinned to the top of your profile page. If not, here's how to pin it.

1. Find the tweet you want to be retweeted.

2. Click on the three dots... right under your tweet.

3. Click on Pin Tweet to page

Now that took 5 seconds. Done!

Comments: "High five on that one ML for letting our readers know. If you're going to play the game you have to know the rules otherwise people will take advantage of you."

Well, Jennifer, everything is out in the open now.

Golden Nugget #63

The Universe's Invisible Sales Force– "Epidemics"

Reading time: 3min 2sec

"I wrote my book without any clear expectation of who would read it, or what, if anything, it would be useful for. It would seem presumptuous to think otherwise." ~Malcom Gladwell

I've been experimenting with ways to deliberately tap into the energy that makes things go viral. That's one of the reasons I wrote How To Gain 100,000 Twitter Followers.

Imagine if you could turn your ideas into something that spread like wildfire?

Marketing scientists have been trying to discover the secret formula for years, but now with advances in technology and the Internet, it opens up new galaxies of possibilities.

I recently read a book by Malcom Gladwell, The Tipping Point. It's a fascinating study into why things spread.

Just as there is an unfortunate Tipping Point for the spread of diseases, there are also "Epidemics"–that create a following CRAZE for ideas, trends, books, movies, social media, and even crime, smoking, drugs, alcohol, suicide, etc.

Gladwell's book delves deep into the phenomena of why and how things go viral–moving from one person to the next, one street corner to the next, one city to the next and from one country to the next.

These "Epidemics"–as we'll call them here, are the Universe's Invisible Sales Force–that carry and distribute everything without thought or concern–leaving participants unaware of what happened.

The Tipping Point occurs when the right energy, elements, circumstances, people, time and place, cross a certain threshold–THEN...the TIP and it affects everyone it touches.

It affects social behavior, health, buying patterns and the way people think. It's an explosion of positivity or complete devastation.

No one can predict or explain its power–why, or how it happens.

It just happens–turning an unknown author into a success, a Fortune 500 company into a fallen empire or an entire country to become stricken by disease.

"We need to prepare ourselves for the possibility that sometimes-big changes follow small events,

and that these changes can happen very quickly. This possibility of sudden change is at the center of the idea behind the Tipping Point and might well be the hardest of all to accept."

The slightest change in circumstance can make the biggest difference, and cause things to tip, for better or worse.

A sudden reversal of fortune can turn your life upside down. Your vision changes–you don't see things in the same way anymore.

This is when your memory of events shift, your capabilities change and what you normally wouldn't have done, now you do.

Look back on your life, and tell me this isn't true?

When situations hit a Tipping Point, something happens–that sends things reeling in the opposite direction, right?

The Tipping Point is a thought-provoking and illuminating book. It gives us a look into the Universe's Invisible Sales Force–"Epidemics" of all types. They are Game Changing occurrences that ensure this fact: businesses and marketers will never be the same. As one reader said, *"Use the thinking in the book to create something new."*

If you want an illuminating rush–read Gladwell's, The Tipping Point. Five Big Stars.

Now if you're wise enough to pick up The Tipping Point, How To Gain 100,000 Twitter Followers and THIS book–you'll have the perfect Trifecta and a knowledge that 99.9 % of Internet users don't have.

It's what I call an unfair advantage.

Comments: Write reviews on books by famous authors and promote your book side by side. If you want to see how I promote the Tipping Point along with my books click here. http://mistersalesman.com/The_Tipping_Point.php *(Scroll down on website)*

Golden Nugget #64

Experiment

Reading Time: 2min 14sec

"All life is an experiment, the more experiments you make, the better."~Ralph Waldo Emerson

I tell you, ole Ralph Waldo Emerson had a different way of looking at things, didn't he?

He's the same guy who said,

"Build a better mouse trap than your neighbor and world will make a beaten path to your door."

I get it, Ralph, believe me, I do. Whether you like it or not, all life is an experiment and since it's an experiment most things you attempt to do are not going to work.

So the more experiments you make, the closer you are to finding things that work.

There is no such thing as FAILURE on experiments. They are just things that either work or don't work.

When you write a book, it's the same thing. Each revision leads you closer to something that will work.

And if you want to do something remarkable, then you must experiment, the better.

If you look at life any other way–Mistakes, Bad Decisions or FAILURES, it will cause you to quit.

This book can help you see things differently and that's what's going to make you a better writer and marketer.

Read and take your time–let the words soak into your brain–it's all a matter of having the right mindset. Nothing more or less–think differently and leave the competition standing in the dust.

Comments: The success in marketing is not the size of your advertising budget, but knowing the real genius 100% comes from inside your head.

Golden Nugget #65

Why Good Marketing Wins Every Time

Reading Time: 2min 2sec

"End with an image~and don't explain"

Stanley Kunitz

I want to clear up the misunderstanding people have about selling and marketing. Most people think that selling is synonymous with marketing, but they're dead wrong.

Selling is the result of a perfectly beautiful equation–quality product + excellent marketing = SALE.

And if you sell before you market it's like putting the carriage before the horse. Marketing makes people aware that your product exists, piques curiosity, and creates desire.

If you sell before you market, you'll sell on price, and you'll end up selling your book for 0.99 cents. Or worse, you'll be tweeting to the world "Download my book for "free."

I know it's painful to hear, but selling before you market will lead to ANXIETY, FRUSTRATION, and for many–the end of a writing career.

Here are 3 things you can do now to

prevent this:

1. Market your product every day: Learn how to write captivating tweets and headlines that arouse curiosity.
2. Find the right words, phrases, sentences that motivate people to action.
3. Study the tweets and headlines of other marketers that get your attention. What made you stop to read more?

Anyway, what you just read is marketing–giving out free information without giving away the ranch–just enough for people to sample your product. And when desire intersects with that special moment in time–a sale is made.

If you want to learn more about building a 100K Twitter platform to launch your products, go here:

getBook.at/HTG100K

Comment: The number one reason people buy is curiosity, and they don't want to be sold. Anyway, good marketing wins every time.

Golden Nugget #66

Ask Me Anything

Reading Time: 2min 2sec

"Should I borrow $5,000 to pay for a marketing seminar? I need to increase my book sales fast."

Everyone wants instant results, and they want them now.

The 3 RULES of Gambling–

- NEVER BORROW MONEY TO GAMBLE

- NEVER BET IT ALL

- NEVER BET YOUR RENT MONEY

Some people learn the HARD WAY–looking for INSTANT PAYBACK.

And when it comes to INVESTING in YOURSELF the same rules apply.

The PAYOFF is often long-term, and if you borrow money, you'll be burdened with debt.

So don't go into debt for high priced books and seminars you can't afford.

That includes the products and services I sell.

Wait until you can afford them, and then dive right in.

You'll learn more than any college education on marketing or social media, but sweet pea, let me say it again–

Wait until you can afford them.

Anyway, if you're not on a tight budget, I bet these books will work for you, or lunch is on me.

HTG100K Dare 2B Great Series

How To Gain 100,000 Twitter Followers

Shorter Sampling Version

The Twitter Secret Key Revealed

Comments: This is a direct marketing piece with some good advice. It will attract people who want to invest in themselves without the burden of debt. Always write with a purpose and a specific market you want to reach. Also, notice the Headline and Hashtags that expand my reach.

Should I borrow $5K for seminar? Ask Me Anything getBook.at/HTG100K #SMM #Twitter #SocialMedia #College #Seminars

Golden Nugget #67

Are You Committing Marketing Malpractice?

Reading Time: 2min 13sec

I see writers, bloggers, and email marketers write posts and at the end of their stories, they never ask for the sales order.

Now that's Marketing Malpractice. By not mentioning and providing a link to your product, you are neglecting to bring the fruits of your labor to fruition. Or, in other words–neglecting to monetize your business.

Your post, filled with useful information was only a sampling of your work to give the prospect a taste of your knowledge and ability.

Then you must specifically direct the prospect how to get your product.

An excellent example is Sam's Club, where you can taste a sample and a demonstrator says, "That also comes in original or rich tangy sauce, and you can buy it right over here in the frozen food section." Now did the prospect find this approach to be offensive?

Of course not, one-way "affairs," those types of 80%/20% relationships never work.

So take heed, provide your link and stop committing Marketing Malpractice.

You owe it to yourself, family, and the customer.

Comments: At the end of every post you should provide a link to your product. The exception is when you're writing a book like this one, it might be misconstrued as too much self-promotion. But for the student it's an excellent way to study the transition from information to offering the product.

Golden Nugget #68

How To Sell Any Product

Reading Time: 4min 50sec

I knew a man who had cockroaches–lots of roaches. One day, he said enough is enough and loaded up his gun and started shooting, one cockroach at a time.

A bullet ricocheted off the wall and killed his neighbor's dog. Then he got into a fight with the neighbor and went to jail for assault and battery and unlawful firing of a firearm. Now he's facing a maximum 5 years in prison.

Pretty bizarre stuff, uh?

Now I have a point, so stick with me.

When I was younger, I did a research paper on roaches. I guess I was fascinated about their existence. Here's what I discovered.

When you see one cockroach, it means you have hundreds, maybe thousands hidden in the walls.

Cockroaches have lived more than 200 million years and predated some dinosaurs.

They have survived everything from floods, earthquakes, insecticides, poisons, droughts, mudslides, fires, to even the atomic bomb.

They are the most adaptable creature on the planet.

- A cockroach can run 3 miles an hour and spread germs and bacteria throughout a home.
- A cockroach can live for seven days without its head.
- A cockroach can hold its breath up to 40 minutes and survive underwater for 30 minutes.
- Newborn cockroaches become adults in less than 40 days.
- There are more than 4,000 species of cockroaches worldwide.
- The American cockroach is attracted to alcoholic beverages, and gets drunk on beer.

I could go on forever, but I respect your time.

Solution?

My friend found it out the hard way. The best solution for roaches is Boric Acid and not store bought products or loaded guns.

Anyway, here's the lesson.

You can sell anything on the internet if you keep this one thing in mind.

Don't try to sell your product first. Tell an interesting story, talk to people about everyday problems and then transition into a solution with a link to your product.

You know the drill by now...

When desire intersects with a moment in time, the right prospects will buy your product.

You're always in the prospect's world when you're talking to them about problems because there is no problem uncommon to man. If they don't have the problem today, they may have it tomorrow.

Like the roaches, you may not have them, but you may have found the story interesting, helpful, and entertaining.

And if the day ever comes that you do have a problem with roaches, or you know someone else that does, you know the solution.

Once you become a storyteller, you'll be able to sell anything on the internet.

And you know what else?

You'll need a social media platform to reach a massive audience.

If you want to learn more, go here:

getBook.at/HTG100K

Comments: Writing a marketing piece every day is an excellent way to offer information, create a bond, build relationships, offer value and sell your products all at the same time. Notice the transition from information to link at the end.

Golden Nugget #69

The On-Line Browser

Reading Time: 1min 12sec

If you want to reach me, the on-line browser, I keep 5 screens open.

I SCAN Everything.
My Attention Span is short.

So don't make me work to READ your book Title Or Headline.

Keep it Short.
It's not what you Think It is.

I LIKE YOU,
But I SCAN Everything.

Comments: This is a short marketing piece to catch the attention of the on-line book browser. Here's the tweet headline. It's not what you think it is... I SCAN everything #TDC NewGenerationof #FearlessWriters #Epic2316 @TheJennieration

Golden Nugget #70

The Secret Sales Formula

Reading Time: 2min 27sec

I get an enormous number of direct messages that I wish I could throw into a bonfire. Most of them are sales messages that violate every principle in the book.

If you're in that camp, I'VE GOT SOMETHING that will help you stand out above the rest.

Draw close and listen.

Years ago, when I was a young man, knocking on doors for a living, my mentor gave me a secret sales formula that I never forgot. (SY+SN+BV+CD=Close)

He said, when you sit down with strangers, the first thing you must do is **SELL YOURSELF**.

- Develop a fun and unique personality.
- Prospects must like you above all else, so it must come from an authentic place of sincerity.
- Then you must get into the prospects world and bond with them. Talk about their family, job, hobbies, and their problems.

- Finally, build your presentation around them: **SHOW A NEED, BUILD VALUE** and **CREATE DESIRE.** Then you're ready to Close the Sale.

Now, you can use the same principles when you write. I don't care what you're writing: tweets, books, headlines, direct messages, or whatever.

You must step into the prospect's world and bond with them. Then pull them into the story. **SY+SN+BV+CD=Close.**

It takes practice to become a great writer. Nobody said it would be easy, but, in the end, it's well worth it.

Golden Nugget #71

Marketing on Multiple Channels

Reading Time: 2min 2sec

In order to sell on the Internet you need to go where the customers are hanging out. That means you must market on multiple channels to reach more customers. I've listed below 24 channels that I operate in. If you are not using these channels, pick out a few to start and add more over time.

1. Twitter followers
2. Automatic Welcome Message
3. TweetJukeBox
4. Hootesuite
5. Hashtags
6. Website
7. Daily Blogs
8. Direct Amazon books
9. Amazon Keywords
10. Keywords Google Search Engines

11. Youtube videos
12. Fiverr Giggs
13. Fiverr Display
14. Backend of Books
15. Testimonials
16. Amazon pay-per clicks
17. Book Reviews
18. Twitter Advance Search
19. Podcasts
20. Instagram
21. Guest blogs
22. Email lists
23. Book Collaborations
24. Guest interviews

Golden Nugget #72

They Just Don't Get It

Reading Time: 2min 14sec

"It seems like everybody's got something to sell. I have five strong arm types following me trying to sell me stuff, I could do without. Any advice?"

Five strong-arm types, uh? Wow, they're putting the MAFIA squeeze on you.

They just don't get it.

PEOPLE DON'T WANT TO BE SOLD–THEY WANT TO BUY.

That's the problem with most users–they don't know what the heck they're doing on Twitter and what makes it worse they're not interested in learning.

TWITTER IS NOT A PLACE TO SELL–IT'S A PLACE TO LAUNCH YOUR PRODUCT.

It's a place where people can TASTE and SAMPLE at no charge, and if they like it, THEY'LL BUY IT.

But twisting arms, roughing people up and burning cars is high pressure, and that kind of selling doesn't work on Social Media.

Anyway, I exaggerate–sometimes–a lot. If you're interested in learning how to build strong and market stronger, go here:

getBook.at/HTG100K

Comments: I'm often asked how I find my topics–one of the best sources is engagement with customers and followers. Any conversation can be turned into useful information, a lesson and a marketing piece that will ultimately lead to increased sales.

Golden Nugget #73

Let's Collaborate

Reading Time: 2min 54sec

Hi, M LeMont I'm captivated by how you write. I think I've read everything on your website: Mistersalesman.com.

I have a plan...

- I want to become a great writer.
- I want to become a great author.
- I want to become a great marketer.
- I want to become a great self-publisher.

And, by the way, I've read all your books and every Golden Nugget you've ever written. You already know from our consultation that I love your unconventional way of writing and getting information out there because it attracts those who are worthy of it–that's how I see it! I write 100 words every day just like you suggested and have felt my writing improve seriously from reading your books and thinking about how I can put myself in a different literary place with my writing.

I think we should Collaborate–I know, styles are super different, right? You may think so but having read as much as I have of yours, I know one thing for sure: We Both Think Outside The Box. What a beautiful mess of contradictions it could be!

You're creative, and so am I. Surely, we can come up with something and even if you don't think so now–I just have a feeling we are meant to someday. So, in the meantime, I will just keep writing.

******

What! Oh, I'm sorry sweetie, No. I work alone. I fly solo. I hate partners. Sorry, I don't mean to un-inspire you, and I can see that you're already a wonderful writer, but I don't do the COLLABORATION thing. It's just not me.

Six months later.... I'm SINGING A DIFFERENT TUNE.

Es como el azúcar a mi alma... like sugar to my soul.

Coming soon my first co-authored book with a brilliant writer and marketer.

Write Like You're Already Famous.

It will turn the literary world upside down.

In the meantime, my latest project: getBook.at/HTG100K

Comments: This was a direct marketing piece to pre-launch the book you're reading now–better than a press release or any paid advertisement.

It was a great way to build a mystery about the co-author without revealing Jennifer's name until it was time.

I wanted to share the post with you for three reasons:

First, Jen slowly showed me something I didn't realize myself–collaborating with the right people encourages personal growth, allows you to dispose of ego & pride–and then get on with making a difference.

Initially, you will have disagreements–and that's okay, but in a good collaborative team, both individuals think and work selflessly, compromising for the sake of the project.

Second, collaborations open up a floodgate of ideas if you are in harmony with your writing partner. Consider the first few weeks like a honeymoon period–getting to know each other.

Working with Jen was truly a joy. It was like food to feed my soul.

Finally, you must find a writing style that suits the team and makes everything flow smoothly. It's the sweet spot and once you find it, the speed in which you write and the rhythm and flow of ideas will astound you.

Now your assignment, if you choose to accept it: Study Chapters 1-4 intensely. This is how you learn to think differently and gain an upper hand over the competition.

Don't be afraid to push the boundaries and explore new ideas on how to write your next book and marketing pieces.

Golden Nugget #74

Review Copy of Your Book

Reading Time: 2min 16sec

Hey, @mistersalesman can I get a review copy of your book? Or would you be interested in making me a case study?"

Well, you're a little late to the party on that one. I tell you, people are always looking for something for nothing.

I tweet A TON of free information every hour that's better than a college degree in Marketing; more than anyone on Twitter–and I would think you would be happy to invest in yourself.

Now I'm about to say something rude, so if you're sensitive cover your ears.

I'm not interested in offering the high-quality content of this book for "Free" any more than Rolls Royce offering its high-end customers a rebate.

You get a nice quality test drive with the sample I provide readers on Amazon, and that's pretty damn good.

I must warn you, the book's addictive, so I've been told–by people who've bought it. They read it and re-read it.

Anyway, with the contents this book provides, it is priced more than fair. I wish I could raise the price, but Amazon takes the lion's share, over $10.00.

The book isn't for everybody; it's for serious minded people who understand and consider the value they get for what they are buying: How To Gain 100,000 Twitter Followers.

Now if you're one of those folks, here's the link: getBook.at/HTG100K

Comments: The post was designed to get rid of the price shopper who only wants something free, while attracting people who know the value of quality information that helps them gain an advantage. Don't be afraid to tell it like it is. In the end, people appreciate the truth.

Golden Nugget #75

How Do I Find My Target Audience Using Your Strategies?

Reading Time 2min 20sec

Jennifer: Your strategies call for following everyone, but how do people find their target audience?

Shouldn't I pick and choose?

Well Señorita, the first thing they (and YOU) should do before you do anything else is gain 100K followers because you need massive numbers to sell your product.

Plus, there is something MAGICAL, in that number. Don't ask me why, there just is. If you pick and choose, then you'll never get 100K. Having a large number of followers, begets more followers and more followers, means more retweets that ultimately result in more sales.

But people want to know: where the heck IS their 'target market?' I originally thought if I followed people doing what I do or liking what I like, I'd be going about it the right way. I saw quickly that was not true.

A lot of those people would do one of two really annoying things. One–they would not follow back and/or Two–they WOULD follow back but NEVER retweet except to say an occasional "Oh, thank you so much for your kinds words and retweets."

I even had some people who insisted you must be part of their group in order to get any retweets from them.

The really ridiculous part was–they weren't some special chicken with a golden egg. They just had some weird-ass pretentiousness that kept their panties all up in a bunch.

Ok, okay… you kill me Jen! So, WHERE DO YOU FIND YOUR TARGET MARKET, right?

They're hidden deep within your follower count. As you continue to increase your numbers, a separation occurs.

Some people will follow while others will unfollow; maybe they didn't like a tweet or a comment you made, but that's a good thing because they weren't your target market.

It goes back to "thinking unconventionally- or outside the box" and realizing that your target market (or followers that matter) are many times not at all who you would envision them to be in your own mind, yeah?

Lastly, Be a good marketer! Intentionally write headlines and posts that attract the right people and repel others.

Comments: The headline was an actual tweet with a link to my website.. Also, notice how each Hashtag is reaching a specific market and from a descriptive sentence. #Twitter #SocialMedia #Authors #Writers #Bloggers #SmallBitz

Golden Nugget #76

M LeMont, are you the most connected person on Twitter?

Reading Time: 2min 19sec

Well, I don't know whether I am or whether I'm not, but I will tell you–I try to connect with everybody I can. That's what Twitter is all about–building lots of casual relationships with the right people who can open doors to new opportunities. As the old saying goes:

It's not what you know that counts but who you know that Matters The Most. Who you know will get you there and what you know will keep you there.

I don't strive to build a lot of deep relationships; IMPOSSIBLE. I can't get deep, because I know I'm going to piss somebody off, and deep relationships hurt when they end. So casual is good for me. And the more followers I have, the more casual relationships I can build.

Recently, the door swung open to Collaborate on a new project that led to a floodgate of ideas. One of which, was the co-author of a soon-to-be-released book, Write Like You're Already Famous.

So the lesson here is: Go out there and build as many casual relationships as you can and see what happens–What do you have to lose?

If you need help gaining followers, go here: getBook.at/HTG100K

Golden Nugget #77

Talk About Fake Followers

Reading Time: 2 min 2sec

"Hey, @Mistersalesman, how can I sniff out fake followers in my Twitter account? I'm sure everybody has some; I just wanna know."

Everybody has their fair share of fake followers, some more than others. Some people buy fake names to boost their following count and to look good on Social Media. But now they're being exposed.

Thanks to TwitterAudit.com, you can run an audit on anybody. If the score is over 65%, then you have a high rating. Here are a few examples:

Lady Gaga twitteraudit.com/Ladygaga

Score 45%/ 23 Million followers/ 28mil Fake

Ellie Goulding

https://www.twitteraudit.com/elliegoulding

Score 82%/4.6 Followers/ 1 million Fake

And of course, I wouldn't dare leave out M LeMont @Mistersalesman.

https://www.twitteraudit.com/MisterSalesman

Score 100%/186,324 followers/975 Fake

Anyway, here's the bottom line: Don't be impressed with someone's follower count. Some people buy followers to boost their image. But the followers are inactive accounts that serve no purpose.

If you want to learn how to grow your followers organically then grab a copy of my latest book. getBook.at/HTG100K

Comments: Now you can know who you are really following. It's a great tool. Plus, buying followers is against Twitter rules and could lead to permanent cancellation of account.

Golden Nugget #78

If It Seems Too Good To Be True, It Probably Is.

Reading Time: 2min 20sec

The truth is hard to find. For example, the other night, I pulled into McDonalds drive thru about 1 am. (I had the munchies, okay?)

Anyway, after I placed my order, I was approached by a very pretty woman who said she just left her boyfriend, and she had no money and no place to stay. She asked if I could take her to my place or a homeless shelter.

I was shocked, and for the first time in my life, I didn't know what to say. I wanted to help her, but in the back of my mind, I knew it was a con game.

Frantically, I weighed the consequences: I could get mugged, robbed, blackmailed, accused of kidnapping, rape, or even worse–someone could get hurt.

You know me by now, *dear reader.*

What did, *I do?*

Or better yet, *what would you do?*

Well, I passed, and I hope you would have done the same thing?

I HAD NO WAY OF VERIFYING HER CLAIM.

Now that sums up the world that we live in. Right? *Right.*

Trust with verification.

And that's one reason, people are hesitant to buy over the Internet because they have been ripped off or they are just unsure whether the product will work as advertised.

I KNOW the feeling because I've changed my mind just before hitting that buy button. I call it pre-buyers remorse.

So, your job as a marketer is to win a prospect's trust, which is done over time.

The average prospect needs to bond with you through your writings, podcasts, videos, etc.

Normally, it takes reading at least 5 posts, before they have enough confidence to buy–then you're no longer a stranger.

Of course, there are those prospects that buy on impulse without the need for any verification because it was something they were looking for or it touched them at that moment.

Anyway, most people are hesitant to buy from strangers–so give them a way to bond with you–through your writings.

And if you want to build a large audience then, go here: getBook.at/HTG100K

Comment: Revising your manuscript is not a formal affair. You can rewrite it as many times as you like until you get it right. Be patient, all you self-publishers–there's no deadline and no pressure except what you put on yourself. So relax and give it all you've got.

Golden Nugget #79

Why Do You Give Away So Much Free Information?

Reading Time: 1min 20sec

It's like getting a college education in marketing without owing SALLIE MAE."

Hey, that's what the Internet is all about– "free information" for anyone who wants to spend the time to find it.

What I try to do is save you time and deliver the content right to your front door.

And...because there's so much competition, the information gets buried under piles of other tweets. So you have to dig to find it.

It's a sample of my work, but it's a damn good sample–so much so, that some people try and make a meal out of it.

Like standing in Sam's Club and eating samples all day. And, that's okay because I never give away the Crown Jewels for free–you have to pay for that.

My goal is to help 100,000 people learn how to use Twitter, any way that I can. So check your

Twitter stream and find the goodies, and implement the ideas.

They will separate you from the crowd. And when you want to graduate from "Free" to "Paid", start here: getBook.at/HTG100K

In the meantime, keep your head to the sky.

Golden Nugget #80

These Aren't The Nerds You're Looking For?

Reading Time: 2min 2sec

No, I'll find the NERDS later, right now I want to talk about the people who send me an onslaught of automated direct messages.

The Auto DM is an unsound marketing tool that's used by unseasoned Twitter users, and it drives me FREAKIN crazy.

Well, it did until I took a closer look, and put it to the "WHAT IF I did this" test.

Let me explain. WHAT IF you sent ONE-TIME a Welcome/Sales message to new followers making them aware of your product, service, or something free for them following you.

Then, WHAT IF you implemented the Six Powerful factors in the book How To Gain 100,000 Twitter Followers, what would happen?

Intriguing. Hey, this might work, or you may get a shit load of unfollows.

According to a study Automated DM on Twitter leads to a 245% increase in unfollow rate.

But there's nothing to worry about because that study didn't include the principles laid down in HTG100k book.

It could be an opportunity to interact and bond with your followers, then they will appreciate the Auto DM.

Since implementing the Auto DM, I've received a lot of favorable responses and the interaction has been fantastic.

I offer to answer any Twitter questions at no charge. After all, who else are they going to call?

It's a soft sales approach and I never mention my product except providing the link in the original DM.

The early sales results are good enough for me to continue using the DM as another Marketing

Channel for reaching and educating people about Twitter.

I would not recommend using the Auto DM if your product or service has a potentially offensive nature that would generate spamming complaints.

The key is to write a direct message that is short and to the point. Ask a question that generates a response. It's an opportunity to bond with new followers before seeing them on Twitter.

Then test, measure results and make adjustments.

Golden Nugget #81

How to Advertise Your Book Like It's on the New York Times Front Page

Reading Time: 2min 2sec

What do you think gets more exposure: a Front Page Ad on the New York Times or a small classified on Craig's List? But of course! –it's the front page of New York Times. That's a No-Brainer.

The last time I checked, The New York Times Front Page Ad: $75,000 a pop, $100,000 On Sundays.

That's cost prohibitive for authors looking to reach a larger audience. Plus, there are no guarantees that you would sell a single book.

But, not to worry. I have something better, and it won't cost you a dime.

I'm going to show you how to display your book on the front page of your Twitter profile and get plenty of exposure.

According to Twitter analytics, I get over 70,000 people visiting my profile every month, and the first thing they see is my book that's pinned at the top of the page. It also makes it easy for people to retweet.

Here's how I did it:

1. Click Home at the top of the main page
2. Click Tweets
3. Find the tweet you want to Pin
4. Click the 3 dots at the bottom of the tweet... Next to LIKE
5. Click Pin to Profile

Comments: When you Pin your book or product, the key is to leave it there for 30 days and measure the number of Likes and Retweets before replacing it. If it delivers the desired results, then leave it there permanently.

Golden Nugget #82

The First 48 Hours Product Challenge

Reading Time: 1min 50sec

Take the book, How To Gain 100,000 Twitter Followers, Secrets Revealed by An Expert, and go to Chapter 12. Now read the first page, and no more.

Apply that one technique, and see how many followers you gain in the first 48 hours. Then tweet your results.

If the results didn't send shock waves of Wow! Holy Shit! this is INSANE! Then I will give you a free consultation session valued at $400.00.

Not enough? More? Selfish, huh?

Okay, here's my 100% product guarantee. I will be your Unreasonable COACH and get you to 100k in less than a year.

And, by the way, four people have already hit 100,000.

@DoriCreates 154,000 @Tableofferings 127,000, @goodsolitaire 124,00, and @17Evolve 108,000.

Remember: If you don't have a Kindle, download the free app for PC, Cell, Tablet.

Now go forth, my esteemed Governor, the book awaits you. getBook.at/HTG100K

Comments: This is a direct marketing challenge to read Chapter 12 and get amazing results in the first 48 hours. When you have a lot of competition in your space and a superior product, then you should offer a product guarantee. The last time I checked, there were over 4,000 Twitter books on Amazon. The ad delivers what it promises and leaves the competition standing in the dust. I promote it twice a day with a link to my Amazon page.

Golden Nugget #83

How to Write a Book that Doesn't Sell?

Reading Time: 2min 2 sec

You think it's easy to write a book that doesn't sell? Well, you didn't think about that before you wrote it, now did you?

C'mon now, don't bullshit me? You had high expectations. You spent hours writing the book with grandiose thoughts of making thousands of book sales. You priced it at $3.99 and then you dropped it to 0.99 cents. Eventually, you gave it away for free.

Free often equated with low value. People won’t read it. Why? Because, the perceived value of anything free is zero. Plus, there's a glut of free books on the market and yours is buried under a pile of other free books.

Are you listening to me?

I'm telling you the undeniable truth. That Freeeee shit doesn't work because it sends the wrong message, not to mention everybody is doing it.

And one last thing–you had the notion that Twitter was the ideal place to sell your book. But it's not. It's not a platform for selling.

No Sir, it's a platform for MARKETING–to offer free information and samples of your work that motivate people to see what else you sell.

Now if you think it's easy to write a book that doesn't sell you're wrong. The Grind, Sacrifice and Long Hours were hard.

So take the time and read all you can about marketing because that's what it's all about.

Comments: Most authors think once they write a book it will sell itself, but just the opposite is true. Book marketing is 99% marketing, and the book is 1%.

Golden Nugget #84

I Want To Thank You

Reading Time: 1min 58sec

I'VE been a lot of places and seen a lot of things, but nothing like this.

I want to thank all my followers, the ones that love me for giving away so much interesting, fun and useful information.

Even the ones who unfollowed and blocked me. I also want to thank the ones that hate me for tweeting so much and being straight up about things.

I want to thank everyone, big, tall, short, skinny, fat, black, white brown, purple, rich and poor...everyone!

Thank you for giving me an endless supply of things to retweet every day. I sure hope I didn't miss anybody, and if I did, I want to thank you too. You Rock!

Golden Nugget #85

"I don't care about no damn 100,000 Followers. Why should I care?"

Reading Time: 2min 29sec

I don't know how my answer would help someone who doesn't know why they should want 100,000 followers, but nevertheless, I'm always willing to help.

Do you keep up with the news? What about the revolt in the Middle East? How were the people united?

Who was the social media authority, influencer, or leader? How did he communicate?

How are Presidential campaigns and elections won? And, how are ideas shared and expanded?

Yes, nowadays, through Social Media. We all a have a role, and we all participate, whether we know it or not. There are two types of people on Twitter: those who want a lot of followers and those who could care less.

If you're the latter, you're probably content being a follower unless put in a situation where you have to be a leader. There's nothing wrong with that.

Everyone can't be a leader, anyhow. Can you imagine if everyone was in charge, what the world would be like?

Anyway, some people just enjoy following others even when the people they follow will never in a million years follow them back and the interaction is all one-sided.

That's fine–if you are fine WITH it! Anyway, there are critically important reasons to want and to HAVE 100,000 followers, and to start you can read about it in my Golden Nuggets.

I took the time to answer your email because it seems like you have a good heart and really wanted to know.

I hope my answer helped. If you want to understand more, then buy How To Gain 100,000 Twitter Followers: Secrets Revealed by An Expert. getBook.at/HTG100K

If you don't have a Kindle, download the free app for PC, Cell, Tablet.

Comment: Write posts that stir up the soul, generate conversations, and offer solutions.

Golden Nugget #86

Why You Should Use Testimonials

Reading time: 2min 58sec

Why You Should Use Testimonials. Ask Me Anything.

I got this message one day from another author,

"Hey M, how are you doing dearest? I see your timeline sparkling with tons of conversations and don't even know how you keep up....! I love your Golden Nuggets–I can't live without them. I hope you're well, you're in my thoughts."

Now that's a good prop, and I'll take it anytime.

When you get a compliment from a person of high esteem, it's like Michael Jordon telling LeBron James, "Hey man that was one hell of game you played."

Now that means a lot more than one of his fans saying the same thing.

Certainly, no offence to fans, but a compliment from a peer or top competitor means so much more.

It was also a testimony that I was compelled to share.

It's amazing how few people use testimonials in their Twitter marketing. It's evidence that people like what you have to offer, or as it's commonly called, 'Social proof'–the number one reason people buy.

People want to know what other people think about your product, not what you think. You can toot your own horn all day, but people will tune you out.

You should use testimonials whenever you can, especially the ones that stand out.

You know the kind that makes you slobber copiously from the mouth.

Get my point?

Testimonials are Social Proof that your product is everything you say it is–Real People, Real Testimonials, Real Results.

Golden Nugget #87

Holiday Gift Time

Reading Time: 1min 8sec

Have you ever bought a gift for someone and they didn't like it?

HOW DID THAT MAKE YOU FEEL?

C'MON, admit it, it made you feel like crap.

You may even felt like hitting them over the head with it.

There's some people you just can't please. Well, I've got a solution.

This year, give everyone a nice book to read.

What! Another FREAKIN book?

Wait a minute...IT AIN'T MY FAULT you gave them the WRONG book.

People love to read "How-To" books. They want to learn new things.

So my holiday books of choice are How To Gain 100,000 Twitter Followers & Write Like You're Already Famous.

And, I'm willing to bet you, after reading these–they will not only thank you–they'll remember you for years to come.

Anyway, here are the links if you want to be thanked profusely this holiday season:

getBook.at/HTG100K

getBook.at/WriteFamous

Hit the gift button.

******

If they don't have a Kindle, they can download the free app for PC, Cell, and Tablet.

Comments: Write a holiday post that is fun and uniquely–designed to make people think about the kind of gift they should buy. Remember, when desire intersects with the right moment in time–a sale is made.

2min 2sec Break

How Will You Rate This Book?

Well, I suppose it depends on who you ask.

But, I bet some will say this is an excellent book and highly recommend it.

Then, there will be some who say–I got several good ideas, and it's well worth the purchase price.

Then others will say, it changed the way I THINK.

While some will say, the authors really pushed the envelope, but I kind of like them anyway.

But here's the killer, 95% won't say anything. That really hurts because we have gotten to know each other pretty well.

I mean, we made a connection. You, me and Jennifer are no longer strangers. After all, you've gotten to know us through our writings, we've been to Macao–and even gotten up close and personal with Robin Leach. (*Ha! remember that guy?)*

We've become like, you know–friends talking and having a cup of coffee at the kitchen table.

So can I be honest with you?

Reviews are the life blood of an author. It's how we keep score, improve, hone our writing skills and breath again.

As Vince Lombardi once said, "I firmly believe that any man's finest hour, the fulfillment of all he holds dear is the moment when he has worked his heart out in a good cause and lies exhausted on the field of battle– victorious."

You may not have thought about it that way, but it's true.

Plus, reviews also help other readers–who rely on your opinion to make an intelligent buying decision.

Yea, I know, and they don't even know you, right?

Anyway, I don't want you to fall into that 95% camp who don't give reviews–I use to be in that camp, it's not fulfilling.

So, here's the deal.

Since you will probably use this book often as a guide, please stop, take 2 min 2 sec and write a review on Amazon and tell everyone how you feel.

And don't forget to register for the free Automated SocialJukeBox consultation and receive free updates to this book. Technology is constantly changing, and I'm always looking for the next big secret.

Send proof of purchase, here: MLeMont.com Click on Contact.

Now, don't worry, Jen and I will be here when you get back–2min 2sec. Then we'll be ready for the last section of Golden Nuggets.

Section 5: RANTS, RAVES, & CAVES

"The cave you fear to enter holds the treasure you seek.

It is by going down into the abyss that we recover the treasures of life.

Where you stumble, there lies your treasure.

The very cave you are afraid to enter turns out to be the source of what you are looking for.

The damned thing in the cave that was so dreaded has become the center where you find the jewel."
~ Joseph Campbell

Golden Nugget #88

I Will Always Love My Mom, She's My Favorite Girl

Reading Time: 2min 25sec

This is dedicated to all the mothers of the world.

"Moms will walk a million miles in their lifetime for their children."

My mother died at 85 of Alzheimer's disease. It was a dreadful disease that wiped out her memory, and all the things she held dear. But, how could she not remember, me?

When I cried, she was always there to comfort me. From diapers, bottles, cooking, daycare, discipline, working, buying groceries, doctor, church, elementary, middle, high school, teachers, homework, practice, sports, college, marriage, grandchildren, counselor, to being my best friend.

I wanted her to know how much I love her. I wanted her to hear me say it one more time.

It was a quiet night as she lay in bed with her eyes closed. She hadn't recognized any of us in a while. My sisters and I sat around her bedside.

Mom opened her eyes and said softly, "Kathy, what are you doing here?"

"Mom I've been here every day taking care of you like you took care of us." Kathy asked, "Do you want me to paint your nails and sing you a song?"

Mom slowly nodded. Kathy sang her favorite song, "Soon and very soon–I'm going to see the Lord." Mom looked up at Kathy with a smile and said, "I love you," closed her eyes and died in my sister's arms.

In a strange way, it was like mom waited for us to get there before she passed away.

Mom today, is your 97th birthday, so I'm writing you this letter to tell you how much I love you, and appreciate the wonderful things you did for me. It's a hard life, and I wouldn't have made it without you. If you could see me, you would be proud. I have a new wife, and things have changed quite a bit since you've been gone.

Veronica, who you loved so much, got enchanted by another man and allowed him to ruin our marriage.

I did what I could–to save our marriage, after catching her in the act. I kept a diary of the separation and divorce for 700 days.

After thirteen years, Veronica asked me to forgive her. I can still feel the pain in my heart that ripped us apart.

You always told me to find the good in people, and do what I can to help someone.

I published a book about the marriage–to help bring closure and to let other people, who may be going through the same thing, know they're not alone.

I will always love you mom, for everything you did for me.

You will always be my favorite girl.

Golden Nugget #89

Do You Have Any Advice on Finding My Grown-Ass Kid a Job?

Reading Time: 2min 2 sec

"Hey, Mistersalesman you said I could ask you Anything. Do you have any advice on finding my grown ass kid a job?"

Yes, I want to talk to parents everywhere.

Parents?

Parents?

Can you hear me?

What is the HOTTEST Job Skill that will guarantee your child finds a job when they graduate from high school or college and get them out of your house?

Yea, I did say–"OUT" your house, didn't I?

Well, the Hottest Job Skill is...

Fluency In A Foreign Language.

The ARMY, NAVY, AIR FORCE, NYPD, State Department, Fortune 500 Companies, APPLE, Amazon, Google, High Tech Companies,

Hospitals, Local Courts and Schools are ALL hiring for Translators or Interpreters.

The Global Market is BOOMING!

I Found 103,000 job posts just for the word Bilingual on Indeed.com

No Shit!!!! That's only ONE related word!

PARENTS–It's time for some Me Time... some Free Time.

Kids of all ages can SPEAK FLUENT SPANISH in 1 year with Jennie at TheJennieration.com.

Comments: This was a direct marketing piece that we ran on Twitter. It provides good information about why learning to speak Spanish is beneficial. It also strikes an emotional chord with parents. The headline draws a lot of attention.

Golden Nugget #90

Men, It's Time to Wake Up!

Reading Time: 2min 29sec

Men, it's time to wake up and give the Women their just due.

I want to talk to all the FELLAS tonight.

FELLAS?

FELLAS?

Are you there?

It's time to give the Women their just due.

They are tired of being pushed around–getting paid less and passed over for key positions.

They have DREAMS and ASPIRATIONS just like you do.

Things are changing.

Inspirational leaders like:

Shonda Rhimes, Creator of TGIT on ABC

Marissa Mayer, CEO Yahoo

Zane, Famous Author

Sonia Sotomayer, 111th Justice of Supreme Court

FELLAS, Are You Listening To Me?

Women are just as smart and powerful as you.

OKAY, It's about to get hot in here. I mean, real Freakin' hot, so I better hurry and say what I have to say.

The days of the quote, "Behind every great man is a woman, ROLLING HER EYES" are gone.

Over.

Done.

Women are no longer your CHEERLEADERS, Babysitters, or Cooks. They are women of power, women of influence and women of strength. They are CEO's, Famous Writers, Authors, Entrepreneurs, Innovators, Twitter Influencers, Surgeons, Pilots, Scientists, Presidential Candidates, etc.

FELLAS, this is your wake-up call!

Over 80% of the nation's direct sales organizations are women.

ONE OTHER THING:

Over 80% of the people that buy How To Gain 100,000 Twitter Followers are: Guess who?

WOMEN!

So FELLAS...

Where does that leave you?

@DoriCreates 150K, @TableOfferings 122K, @17Evolve 105k

getBook.at/HTG100K

Golden Nugget #91

Go Ahead, just Wonder

Reading Time: 3min 5sec

There's nothing like writing creatively with a partner. When I found mine, I felt the blending of two souls and the music of our mutual composition.

Harmony

Synchronicity

NOTHING like it.

I had my own mind, but now–the mind of another too.

Ideas appear like an endless flow~~

...Sweet-spots

One phrase may be all it takes to make the energy emerge.

Our words collide forming silent powerful explosions of ineffable beauty and precision.

These moments–I imagine a tandem walk, perfectly balanced on a tight rope, high above the mess below.

Even in the deep-dark silence of my solitary night, it feels like 'stepping out into the sun.' The illumined thought produces words that glide onto my page effortlessly and radiate all that is within.

Can you feel that light?

I send my words through space and time to be caught by my writing partner in the morning.

The whole process swings back around.

I read my partner's writings and say, "Swing me all of your light…" through the LIVEWIRE.

I ponder and I feel again the silent explosion of our words and ideas effortlessly colliding to create something that otherwise would not exist.

Sometimes I say aloud, "I've been outta my mind today–only gonna 'find the higher low'.

I just need to hide from myself and my words until tomorrow."

He says, "I'll lift up–carry the load!"

That's when I know.

I know where I've got to go.

And I say, "Can you hold me when I fall from the lines?"

I'm going there too...

'Down

down

deep down'

...INTO the WRITER'S ABYSS.

We'd been Writing Solo…but Now…

We're the LIVEWIRE! Oh Wonder~ Inspired by Collaborative Singer-Songwriters

Golden Nugget #92

When people call you out in public.

Reading Time: 3min 10sec

What should you do when people unfollow and try to tarnish your good name by calling you out in public?

Well, the first thing is don't PANIC, take a deep breath, count to ten in Spanish; uno, dos, tres, cuatro, cinco...

Then realize that it has nothing to do with you.

The reason they threw you under the bus and called you a lame duck has to do with their belief system; what they were taught, read, heard and saw. Even the people they came into contact with influenced them more than their parents.

So you don't have anything to do with how they feel inside about what you tweeted. They're a ticking time bomb, waiting for something or someone to cross their path.

Take, for example, this nice guy who wanted to let all of Twitter world know that he unfollowed me.

"Pfffff just turned you off, spam your own Twitter page. Lame posts as well."

Well, the first thing I did was retweet his message, you know to kind of help get the word out, I mean that's what he wanted, right?

Then I replied, "Everyone is having so much fun. But I heard there's another party more your style around the corner.

Take care and thanks for the time we shared." Anyway, the moral of the story, think before you Tweet.

Remember, there's nothing wrong with you. And, if you want to know more then buy How To Gain 100,000 Twitter Followers, there's an entire chapter dedicated how to engage in heated conversations. getBook.at/HTG100K

Bye, for now.

Comments: If you're not pissing someone off, on Twitter then you are playing it too safe. Go out there and be the host of your own talk radio show – make it fun, entertaining and informative.

Golden Nugget #93

It's Only After You've Lost Everything That You're Free To Do Anything.

Reading time: 1min 55sec

It's the man or woman that have nothing to lose that everyone should worry about.

In the beginning, the founders of Google, Twitter, Apple, and Amazon had nothing to lose.

And now they have to worry about people like you.

If you're already broke, rejected, and humiliated, then it's time to get your reward.

Nobody said it will be easy, but in the end, it will be well worth it.

Learn how to win friends and influence people, then change the world.

Comments: Command the readers attention with a powerful headline that will make them read the very first line. i.e. "It's the man or woman that have nothing to lose that everyone should worry about." Now, if that's you, then let your writing reflect your freedom to express yourself–experiment and find a brand new world.

Golden Nugget #94

Favor & Reciprocity? Ask Me Anything

Reading Time: 2min 54sec

The anonymity of the Internet gives some people a false sense of confidence, the same way alcohol affects the brain.

But if you violate professional protocol, 'Sales 101' before you get to know someone then you might get thrown under the bus.

It's like this guy who sent me a direct message, *"Hi @Mistersalesman, I need an urgent favor from your side. Please reply to me if you can help me."*

I never had a single conversation with this person or read any of his tweets. You know the kind.

My response?

1. Well, I hate to give good people bad news, and you are a good person, I am presuming but at this point all I can say are two things:

1. Who the heck are you? We've never even spoken before and you're asking for a favor?

2. I have plenty of things I need, but I don't go around asking complete strangers!

> Get to know me through my work. Let me get to know you through yours; and in time maybe ask me again. How's that sound?

Anyway, like I said, at this point, that's all I have to say about it –other than…Really??

If you want to learn how to market on the internet, get my latest book How To gain 100,000 Twitter Followers so you won't be like this poor soul who had no clue how to sell.

Bye, for now.

Comments: Notice the actual tweet headline with a wonderful string of Hashtags that formed sentences to describe the message. Favor & Reciprocity? Ask Me Anything. getBook.at/HTG100K #Twitter #Smallbiz #GainMoreFollowers #SMM #Entrepreneur You can use emails, conversations and DM's to write an intriguing story. Then use a transitional phrase to offer the product link.

Golden Nugget #95

Own It!

Reading Time: 2min 2sec

Ladies…

Ladies…

Don't you get tired of always hearing:

Women are SO COMPLICATED?

Come on–I mean REALLY!?

Let's "Work That Word" ~POOF!~

"Magical Wordsmithing"

- Intricate & Involved
- Impenetrable & Confident

YOU SEE WHAT I MEAN?

Now you SEE it, Right?

Those guys have got it ALL WRONG…again!

It's YOUR TIME NOW!

Are you processing what I am saying to you??

Take it, own that word!

Redefine it for them…PROPERLY!

"You're the boss right now.

This is your game and you better come to play!

You used to hold your freak back, now you're letting go. Making your own choice...

Let them say you're complicated. That you must be outa your mind. They've had you underrated!!"

Some words of Demi Lovato...

Now Go! OWN "your crazy,"

Own "your freaky", Own your off the hook Confidence!"

Write about it! Live it! Love it!

If it's in you, let it fly!

Get out your comfort Zone!

Comments: Thanks, Jennifer–simply brilliant! And as Shonda Rhimes said in her book, The Year of YES: "You must learn how to become 'Badassery'–owning your gifts and accomplishments.

Or "go stand tall in the sun & in full view of the world–dance it out & (superwoman) power-pose like crazy!"–live your life with SWAGGER, and don't give a crap what anyone else thinks about it.

"The woman I see may be new, but I know her well. I love her..." She's ME!

Now I think what Shonda was really saying:

Don't Write To Be Famous, Write Like You're Already Famous.

Golden Nugget #96

A Quote Can Make it Simple & Easy

Reading Time: 2min

"What are you doing to reduce your cognitive overhead?"

It's a phrase used by Amazon founder Jeff Bezos, referring to the number of decisions or actions readers must make before they can actually buy the book they want.

There are way too many steps involved in buying an ebook–so most first-time buyers say, "Forget this mess!"

Here's the biggest problem:

Did you know that 85% of users tweet using a mobile device?

Plus, 75% of them don't have a Kindle and don't know they can download a FREE Kindle app for PC, Cell, or Tablet.

So what are you going to do to reduce your cognitive overhead?

Take action, inform others and make them aware. Retweet this link every day until the COWS crow and the CHICKENS moo!

You have the power to make a difference, and who knows, one day somebody might say THANK YOU for the tip.

Comments: Notice how the post was built around Jeff Bezos' quote and evolved into some valuable information. I get many people who thank me for telling them to download the free Kindle reading app. "I didn't know, thanks so much."

Golden Nugget #97

Goolge Plus 25K Can I Make Money

Reading Time: 4min

I have a Google plus community of 52,000 members. Can I make any money from this or is it a waste of my time?

Here's what I have to say. You are competing with millions of people who want the same thing and are vying for the same eyeballs.

What does that mean? Everybody wants instant success, but they're not willing to pay the cost to be the boss.

Expectations are free, but the cost of success is expensive.

You must put 10,000 hours in the shortest possible time, for it to have the greatest impact.

You must acquire knowledge & know-how, and turn it into action.

You must be willing to learn from the best, those who have gone ahead of you and already proven their results.

You must master the rules, and then you must break them like a pro.

Now I hate to give people bad news, especially when they mean well, but you asked me a question, and I'm not going to blow smoke up your nose to give you an adrenaline rush.

I'm going to tell you the truth and give you the facts. Your 52K members on Google Plus is nothing if you stop there.

The money you earn is commensurate to what you know.

If you make meager wages then that is what you deserve, and nothing more.

But the more you develop your skills, the more money you'll earn.

Now that's about all the free advice I can give you in one message, but IF you want to learn more buy How To Gain 100,000 Twitter Followers getBook.at/HTG100K

And, if you don't, buy it, I understand, believe me, I do. Take care.

Comments: Take emails and turn them into raving posts so everyone can benefit. Readers will look forward to reading your posts every day and dig to find them.

Golden Nugget #98

You Have To Know What You've Got

Reading Time: 3min 14sec

Wow, you have a lot of followers. I'm still trying to figure this out. Can you give me some advice?

Sure, I'll be glad to. The first thing you should do is–know what you've got.

Here's what I mean...

I knew a man who bought a ranch and discovered hidden, deep on the land, a bunch of crazy ass chickens.

There were hundreds, maybe thousands of them with different colors, sizes, species, and personalities.

Some were nice chickens, moody chickens, mean chickens, and even chickens that loved to fight.

But the man wasn't impressed; he despised the commotion and the mess those chickens made every day.

So, then one day, he discovered an array of eggs: white, red, blue, green, yellow and pink– the males had laid these eggs.

The man had never seen or heard of anything like that before.

He had a collection of rare chickens that was worth millions.

Now the same is true about Twitter–you have to know what you've got before it means anything to you.

Twitter is more than updates.

Anyway, I tweet a ton of free information every hour, but "free" can only take you so far.

If you want to know the deep, hidden secrets how to gain 100K followers, then buy my book How To Gain 100,000 Twitter Followers, Secrets Revealed by An Expert getBook.at/HTG100K.

Comments: Write with a specific purpose: to create curiosity, desire, bond, inspire, motivate, educate, and build confidence. Remember...when desire intersects with a unique moment in time a sale is made. So write a new post every day.

Golden Nugget #99

What I Learned From Albert Einstein Over Dinner

Reading Time: 3min

One of my favorite pastimes is studying the works of Albert Einstein, here are 10 things I learned from one of the smartest men that walked the planet, and I learned it–while eating dinner.

1. The greatest inventor is "Accident." THINK ABOUT IT!
2. Experiment every day. I REFER to it as prospecting for gold.
3. If the results are amazing and swift, then stop and pour all your time and resources into the project.
4. Always ask yourself the question: What if I do this, what would happen?
5. Don't overlook the obvious, the answer could be staring you right in the face.
6. Stay curious and see how deep the rabbit hole goes. Many times it's a dark hole that goes nowhere, and you must reject the project quickly and move on to

something else. Test, reject, and test again. Keep testing.

7. Stay open-minded, and you'll find new gems of opportunity you weren't looking for.

8. Don't worry about the results. 10,000 experiments with no results were not failures; they were the steps that led you to the right result.

9. Never Quit.

10. Keep Prospecting for Gold Every Day

Anyway, by applying the 10 steps, I discovered the strategies in the book HOW To Gain 100,000 Twitter Followers. Learn more here: getBook.at/HTG100K

Comments: A real writer is like a cop, he's always on duty looking for something to write about. There is never a shortage of topics.

Golden Nugget #100

Why First Attempts Make You Feel Like An Idiot

Reading Time: 2min 2sec

Remember the first time you tried riding a bicycle. What happened?

What about the first steps you took as a baby? Well you may not remember those but ...the first day on a new job? And, what about the first book you wrote?

Or your first date?

I bet you screwed them up royally. First attempts are hard, awkward and make you feel like an idiot. This is why most people are reluctant to try anything new.

They didn't know the real secret of riding a bicycle or taking those first baby steps. FIRST ATTEMPTS FAIL.
Now this is true, not just some of the time, but almost all the time. So don't feel badly, embarrassed or lose your confidence. TRY THINGS AT LEAST TWICE before giving up (more than twice is better). Practice makes perfect.

The second attempt will be much easier than the first by a WIDE MARGIN. And the more attempts you make beyond two, the better the odds you will succeed.

Sometimes, it's the obvious things that make the biggest difference.

When you have nothing to lose and everything to gain, why not try. Nothing beats a failure but a try. TRY again, and again and again.

I think you get the point.

Anyway, check out HTG100K @Doricreates and @Tableofferings, they tried it one more time to gain 100K Followers and succeeded. Here's the link: getBook.at/HTG100K

Comments: Write about life experiences and it will help inspire others and people will appreciate it. We all go through the same bullshit–there's no problem that is uncommon to man.

Golden Nugget #101

I Want To Ask You A Bunch of Questions!

Reading Time: 2 min 2 sec

My favorite pastime is watching movies. I remember every memorable scene I've ever watched.

Do you remember, Kindergarten Cop starring Arnold Schwarzenegger as Detective John Kimble?

He's a plain clothes detective holding a gun on a criminal in a store, when a security guard rushes in, "Freeze, drop the gun."

"I'm Detective John Kimble–I'm a cop, you idiot!"

Okay, so what's my point? I didn't haul you in here to tell you that. Well, my point is this: If you are a writer, author or anything else that involves storytelling then there's an awful lot you can learn from watching movies.

Now let me show you how I would promote one of my books using a spin from Kindergarten Cop–speaking in a Russian voice and sounding just like Arnold.

"I'm a Social Media expert, and I want to ask you a bunch of questions! What are you trying to accomplish on Twitter? How many followers do you have? Do you want more? Then why haven't you bought my book, How To Gain 100,000 Twitter Followers? Come on, don't bullshit me, everyone wants followers! Let me help you, even Steve Jobs and Michael Jordan had coaches.

Don't be ridiculous–just do what I tell you! Buy the book, and get the Free 1 on 1 consultation. Hurry, do it now before you make me mad!"

Alright, you got it? There's nothing new under the sun. Being creative is a matter of connecting the dots, seeing something different in what already exists.

Steve Jobs, said Apple was a shameless thief, but he was ready to sue if he caught someone stealing from him. Go figure?

Comments: When you're in writing mode, always be ready to write down ideas, they won't wait on you.

Golden Nugget #102

Nothing Is Impossible For A Man, Who Refuses To Listen To Reason ~Gary Halbert

Reading Time: 2 min 2sec

Now, that's a powerful quote that gets my creative juices flowing. Imagine what you could discover if you refused to listen to reason, or if you refused to follow the herd.

Is the majority always right or is it just a safe place to hide from criticism and rejection?

Well, one thing is for sure, if you follow the majority, you will get the same results as everyone else.

So don't rack your brain to figure out why someone is getting better results than you. It's simple; he's doing something different.

Einstein, put it this way, "The definition of insanity is doing the same things repeatedly, and expecting different results." The bottom line? Don't be afraid to go against popular opinion or beliefs.

"Just because that's the way we always did it," isn't good enough. And if I were you, I wouldn't subscribe to that way of thinking. Dare To Be DIFFERENT leads to GREAT THINGS.

Golden Nugget #103

Do I Need To Treat All My Followers The Same Way?

Reading Time: 2min 10sec

Who deserves your time and attention? Do you treat all your followers the same? Now I want you to think about that before you answer.

Your first reaction would be "YES, of course, I do."

Then you are treating most of them wrong.

"What! How dare you say something like that, you don't know me."

Well, I know enough to tell you that all your followers don't deserve to be treated the same way.

You have some followers who retweet your books and others who retweet a pretty quote or what you had for lunch. Then you have followers who don't retweet at all.

And what about those followers who buy your books and those followers who could care less about your book, even on launch day.

Now, you see it would be unfair to treat all of them the same.

That's why I treasure retweeters and anyone who buys my books. I Got You. I'm All Yours!

There is real meaning when somebody tells you "I got you–I'm all yours". It means: I've got your back.

I'm from the old school of marketing, where you make the customer feel important. Some rules don't change even on social media.

We're all vying for the same eyeballs so get on the bandwagon and treat your retweeters and fans special, or you could be left behind.

Golden Nugget #104

I Am Thankful For All Who Said No To Me

Reading Time: 2min 2sec

You made me stronger, and you made me a better writer, and a better thinker.

To everyone who told be no, (you know who you are) Thank you.

First They Will Laugh, Next They Will Applaud, Then They Will Copy And Finally They Will Shout:

"Hey, that's my boy, that's my neighbor, that's my friend; I knew him in college, we were roommates. I always knew he could do it; he was always smart. Different... you know what I mean?"

Yea, I know what you mean.

Now listen to me, if I can do it, you can too! You must keep on, keeping on. Never give up, never.

Comments: Sometimes it's good to write a motivational piece that inspires someone to keep on, despite obstacles and adversities--without a link to your product or book.

Golden Nugget #105

What's your name?

Reading Time 2min 20sec

"So it's @MisterSalesman, but it's Bobbi Dixon...where does M LeMont come in?"

I get that question a lot. A few years ago, my business partner suggested that I start a blog and teach people how to sell, so we bought the domain mistersalesman.com.

Later, I opened a Twitter account. I couldn't decide what picture to use, but wanted something that stood out, so I used a picture of a woman and a manly handle @mistersalesman. What a crazy combination.

At the time, I was too busy working on the website. (Writing a gazillion posts.) The Twitter account sat idle for a few years until I wrote my first book. Then I realized that the book wasn't going to sell itself just because I wrote it. So I made my way back to Twitter and found that it was simple, but yet complicated and nobody knew how to use it.

Jennifer: Ah ha! So, you got yourself into that "beautiful mess of contradictions" quite literally! Hahaja! Oh my gosh! (laughing)

You got it baby! And I figured I better make it look pretty!

After cracking the code, the account took off like a rocket. The @mistersalesman handle and the picture of the pretty blonde became a terrific branding campaign; sort of like Ronald McDonald or Geico gecko commercials.

You always have a way of bringing a smile, don't you! There's one small difference: those 'branding campaigns' have no mystery associated with them. I get the association part~ people associate "blondie" with @mistersalesman (laughing) as odd as it is—cool too! But, no one knows WHO the REAL MAN is "atrás" the image....(behind it all).

Jen, I don't think anybody cares but you. Now nobody knows, but you.

Anyway, some seven books later, it's time to link @mistersalesman to my books and my name M LeMont. Now that's the skinny of it. I wish I had more to tell you.

Golden Nugget #106

Negative People. Have No Fear.

Reading Time: 2min 2sec

It all comes down to you.

Now listen closely, I have something to tell you: Your thoughts are dancing away from you.

They light up the sky at night. I can see them. They're thoughts of doubt and fear. I passed by, and heard them say you can't do it.

STAND BACK. What do they know? Have they ever tried it? I've been there. I know how it feels. Their words cut deep.

They'll grab your heart and run. Then it takes hold of you. You stop dreaming, stop believing. You become one of them.

NO FREEDOM, NO PURPOSE.

Do you hear me?

I'm trying to tell you, it all comes down to you. You've had enough and taken a lot.

It's time to walk away from them. Have no fear. Stand Up, Throw a Finger in the air and Walk Away.

Take a breath, grab another one, and BREATH. Keep breathing. BREATH. You can do it.

It all comes down to you.

Golden Nugget #107

"Don't Eat The Cake Elli Mae."

Reading Time: 2min 2sec

There's never a dull moment if you follow @Mistersalesman. My follower, AKA Clyde complained that nobody followed him from the RT Follow lists. He tweeted,

"SCAM! @Mistersaleman told me to buy his book and find out why."

Well, that was almost true. I told him: if you want to play the game then you must know the rules.

Otherwise, don't complain if people don't want to follow you.

There could be a lot of reasons why people don't follow you, and the book will explain. And with that, he swore on everything holy that the RT TRAIN lists were a SCAM to buy my book.

Then another follower tweeted:

"I hit 5000 followers in 1 month! #So Excited! Try it out: getBook.at/HTG100K

Anyway, after several rounds of just plain nonsense, with the other follower, I offered to refund his $5 subscription and remove him from the Retweet Train. He rejected my offer. **He wanted more**–he wanted me to wave a magic wand.

The Bottom line? "Don't eat the cake, Elli Mae." In other words, do whatever you can to satisfy your customers, but don't kiss their ASS, wash their clothes, and cook their food. You can't satisfy everybody.

Golden Nugget #108

How to gain more followers by hanging dirty laundry on a clothesline

Reading Time: 2min 2sec

"Mistersalesman, you retweeted a picture of some dirty laundry, but in all honesty, they were dirty underwear hanging on a clothesline, so I unfollowed and blocked you. That was several months ago, and then recently I read a nice post you wrote and was impressed. I said maybe he's not a bad guy after all. I'm glad I found you again, and thanks for all the free information."

Ooooh! My! My! Now that's a real testimony. I'm glad that the follower found their way back and saw the infotainment value in what I tweet.

I don't retweet vulgar pictures unless it has some funny caption that makes the picture hilarious.

And that leads to my point. Did you know that 50% of users view your time-line before they make a decision to follow?

They want to see the content you're tweeting and also your profile.

I'm very selective what I tweet and retweet because I want to provide high-quality content, and that's why a lot of people follow the RT Train.

So think before you tweet and if you make a mistake delete and try again. Nobody's perfect.

Golden Nugget #109

The UNFORGIVING...Who are they?

Reading Time: 2 min 2sec

The Unforgiving?

They are people who are quick to judge--

You know the kind?

They are the first who cast the biggest stone when you make a mistake.

Like making an ERROR in your self-published book. You would think the world had ended.

I mean, it's not like jumping out of a plane and your parachute, not opening.

It's not like you made a corporate mistake and had to lay-off everyone at your company because you couldn't meet payroll.

No, it's nothing like that.

So Relax-- Don't let the UNFORGIVING get under your skin.

Whatever the mistakc--

You can fix it.

You can make it better!

Of course, it helps if you have a guide that tells you the SECRETS about how to make YOUR BOOK better--long after you publish.

Read this book over and over again.

THINK DIFFERENTLY AND LEAVE THE COMPETITION STANDING IN THE DUST.

Comments: You have an enormous advantage over 99% of the competition who have not read and may never read this book.

Golden Nugget #110

You came out of NOWHERE...

Reading Time: 2min 3sec

Who are you??

My Amiga Aficcionada continued...

"ML You're workin', buidling a MYSTERY... & choosing everything sooo CAREFULLY."

You got me screamin' at your strangeness...&

then sayin' "Where's that POST by LeMont?"

"I only bet you don't sleep at NIGHT, thinking of the next words...building that MYSTERY...and that nice-lookin' blonde...your "photo"...ok "Bobbie Dixon! Brilliant Marketing or just...a Facade?~ I'm going to find out!"

Well you got me, I'm going on the journey.

And as the song goes...you know it-

"Yea your working', building a mystery...you're a beautiful f-'ed-up man with an edge and charm."

Shit...I think she's got me figured out!

And for the record...she better know:

I don't "wear sandals in the snow!"

Now that sounds like someone who has studied everything I've written. I know she has, in fact!

If you want to be a great writer/marketer, then you must STUDY the WRITINGS, STRATEGIES, QUIRKS and UNIQUENESSES of great writers and marketers.

So that's why I co-authored this book with a brilliant writer...to show everyone HOW to write "without your SHADOW getting in the way!"

Don't Write to Be Famous, Write Like You're Already Famous.

Golden Nugget #111

When You Hit Rock Bottom, it's Time to Celebrate.

Reading Time: 2 minutes 4 seconds

When you hit rock bottom, it's time to Celebrate.

"It's been three years, and I'm way down on your list.

Don't treat me like I'm a puppet on a string.

Don't talk to me like you think I'm dumb.

I got dreams and aspirations like you do.

LIKE I SAID... I don't care what you think

You can't control me."

******

Why? Because!

When you hit rock bottom, it's time to Celebrate.

The good news nothing's permanent and everything changes.

The same people you meet going up, you'll meet them again coming down. That you can count on.

DRY YOUR EYES

WIPE AWAY YOUR TEARS

In life, we have to put up with so much BULLSHIT but don't give up.

Your day will come... just be ready.

I Know What I Am Talking About!

When that day comes, KNOCK, KNOCK open the door and just smile. It's time to CELEBRAR! CELEBRATE!

Until then... Don't Write To Famous, Write Like You're Already Famous.

Golden Nugget #112

Can You Handle The Truth?

Reading Time: 2 min 14sec

"Now you've co-Authored a book, can you please explain how you REALLY feel about COLLABORATIONS?"

"I'LL ANSWER THE QUESTION."

"YOU WANT ANSWERS?"

"I think I'm entitled to them!"

"YOU WANT ANSWERS?!"

"I want the truth!"

"YOU CAN'T HANDLE THE TRUTH!!"

******

That was a quote from the movie, A Few Good Men

That's the way I feel:

Flying Solo to…co-authoring a new book.

The best damn thing I ever did!

You want the truth about Collaborations?

Then, here you go, I'll give it to you.

COLLABORATING IS A LANDMINE THAT CAN LEAD TO A GOLD MINE!

- If you can fight through your own pride, ego and self-will…

- If you can understand another person's point of view and writing style

- If you can set aside the bullshit that keeps you shackled inside your own opinions…

Then it can lead to a Flood Gate Of Ideas That will Astound You!

It took us two weeks to find that GOLDMINE.

Now WE have created something truly remarkable–Different than any Non-Fiction–How To Book ever written! The contrasting styles will tantalize you like salt and sugar and have you begging for more.

Comments: Never say Never! Don't be afraid to think differently than you thought before, even if it makes you uncomfortable. This could be your compass guiding you to your best self, your best place, your best life.

Golden Nugget #113

To Thyself Be True–Lucky Breaks

Reading Time: 2min 18sec

"People who succeed at the highest level are NOT LUCKY; they're doing something differently than everyone else." Tony Robbins

Sorry, Tony, but I'm going to have to disagree with you.

Here's why–it's that word Luck. Everybody's Lucky somehow. You're Lucky God opened your eyes to see the sun rise! Or maybe that you made it back home for dinner.

I mean, there are LUCKY BREAKS in virtually everything.

They play a major role in the success and failure of any business. Just ask an HONEST business owner to tell you the truth about their experiences that got them to the top.

Most people want to take credit for their success, and make you believe it was their superior INTELLECT OR TALENT that caused them to rise to the top. But it was that Lucky Break that got them there– meeting the right person, timing, or being in the right place or situation.

So I'd rather have a LUCKY BREAK, than being good–any day.

Life is a game of inches, and we'd like to take credit for it all, but what has the LAST word? Is it LUCK? To Thyself Be True.

Golden Nugget #114

How Do I Become Visible on Twitter?

Reading Time: 2min 10sec

That's easy–Trade in everything you thought you knew about Twitter for these SIX Powerful Factors.

I mean it from the depths of my heart! This is what you have to do... no matter what anybody else tells you, do these Six every day.

1. Tweet
2. Retweet
3. Follow
4. Unfollow Non-Followers
5. Engage
6. Follow Back

The MORE PROFICIENT you become at doing those Six Factors, the more VISIBLE you'll be on Twitter.

Stay True To The Process And The Process Will Stay True To You.

Lay down the tracks–gain 100,000 Followers.

And, by the way, there is one more important secret you must do.

Learn more, here: getBook.at/HTG100K

Golden Nugget #115

Launch Day

Reading Time: 2min 2sec

"Heads up! Heads up!

Here's another one!

And a... and a....another one.

Yeek yeek woop woop! why you all in my ear?!

Talking a whole bunch of shit

That I ain't trying to hear!" ~Ludacris

Count Down to Launch Day

Write Like You're Already Famous

Oh my goodness, hold on a sec! Whooo, the jet is swaying a bit too much for my comfort.

Wait.

What?

Can't you see I have to get to Macao?

Exclusive interview with M LeMont

- Marketing

- Writing
- Self-Publishing

Comments: Take a few lines from movies and songs and make a fun and entertaining marketing piece that can be used for years to come.

Golden Nuggets #116

You'll Never Become A Great Writer If You Give Up

Reading Time: 2min 2sec

Recently, I watched one of my all-time favorite movies, The Five Heartbeats.

There's a memorable scene in it, where you can learn a thing or two.

Donald "Duck" Matthews spoke to the audience at an Awards Ceremony: I was at a party once, and a critic said–

"DONALD MATTHEWS IS GOING TO BE A GREAT WRITER WHEN HE SUFFERS MORE."

Well, I'm on my way to becoming a great writer and I have two people to thank–my fiancée Tonya and my brother JT. My brother...who's been the same selfish m****f***a since we were kids!

Now tell me, dear reader, if that didn't get your attention?

Life uses everything to test your sincerity.

No matter what you're going through, one thing is for sure–you will never become a great writer if you give up.

Adversity makes you stronger–smarter and is a great teacher. It won't leave you alone until it teaches you the lesson it wants you to learn.

Success, on the other hand, teaches you very little that will help you grow, and if you're not careful, it will become your enemy.

I wish I could tell you more, but *I'll leave it at that for now.*

Golden Nugget #117

Think Outside The Box

Reading Time: 2min 2sec

How many times have you heard the cliché, to be creative, to be inventive, to be successful, "You must THINK OUTSIDE THE BOX?"

Probably enough times to make you sick– plus, it doesn't do anything for you.

Well, here's the problem.

HOW CAN YOU THINK OUTSIDE THE BOX WHEN YOU'RE INSIDE THE BOX?

You must transform your mind while you're inside the box before you can THINK OUTSIDE THE BOX.

Does that make sense?

So the first order of business–learn to THINK DIFFERENTLY THAN EVERYONE ELSE.

And that's what we've tried to convey through out the pages of this book. Let it be a guide– read it over and over again.

It will transform your mind, and you'll start seeing things differently. A spoon will no longer be a spoon.

You'll find new uses and new ways to write, market, package, and repackage things. The same old stuff, but with a different twist and a different meaning.

There is nothing new under the sun.

Golden Nugget #118

Be You and Do It Your Way

Reading Time: 2min 2sec

"Yes, There Were Times, I'm Sure You Knew, When I Bit Off More Than I Could Chew.

But Through It All, When There Was Doubt, I Ate It Up And Spit It Out.

I Faced It All And I Stood Tall;

And I Did It My Way."

That quote is from Frank Sinatra, 'My Way.'

I dedicate that song to everyone who has been knocked down and gotten up just one more time, refusing to give up.

For all the BRUISES, PAIN and HURT

For all the times that NOBODY believed in you.

It's Finally Your Time.

Don't Write To Be Famous, Write Like You're Already Famous

New Generation of Fearless Writer s

The Think Different Crowd

Thank you for taking this journey with us.

"Every life needs another life.

Every Heart needs another Heart.

Every day is a new day." Kem

Conclusion

P.S. Two Questions & A Bonus

We would like to ask two questions:

1. How would you rate this book on a scale of 1 to 5 with five being the highest?
2. Why did you answer the first question the way that you did? (Please expound a bit.)

Please go to MLeMont.com and

- Click the blue contact button to view the questions.
- Type your answers in the box. Your reply will help improve the next edition of this book.
- Your positive response to our book via Amazon's Review Page supports us tremendously as authors. So, please simply copy and paste your answers onto Amazon's review page. This is the greatest compliment you can give authors because your reviews help sell our books.
- Finally–Once you've completed your review on Amazon, send the confirmation code to M LeMont and set up your free consultation

HOW TO AUTOMATE YOUR TWITTER MOST EFFICIENTLY along with any questions you might have about the book.

Post Remarks

Publisher: "Okay, so let me get this straight? Collaborating is like having ONE eternal orgasm..."

No, No, No.

That's not what it's like.

Well, not exactly.

Writing a book with a coauthor was more like 1+1 Equaling FOUR, FIVE, SIX, or SEVEN.

Like constant mind jolts–chemistry–energy that lifts you higher.

IT'S A FEELING I WISH EVERYONE COULD EXPERIENCE.

"Everyone, ML?"

Yes, everyone, even you, sir!

Thank you again, for your time and attention. We hope you learned a lot and enjoyed the journey as much as we did.

Other Books & Services by M LeMont

HTG100K Dare 2B GR8 Series

Book 1 Basics: How To Use Twitter: From Cradle To Grave

Book 2: How To Gain 100,000 Twitter Followers, Secrets Revealed An Expert

Book 3: Write Like You're Already Famous

New Series Rants, Raves, & Caves

Book 1: Little Book of Big IDEAS

Short Story Books

As Fate Would Have It

These Eyes Have Scene

Novels

Harry's Love Letters Hacked!

Shh! Kiss Me Baby

M LeMont Caught Up What's Done In The Dark Comes To Light

Hot trailer

https://www.youtube.com/watch?v=dU_WYDGXQ9U&feature=youtu.be Google Search: Caught Up - What's Done in the Dark Comes to Light

Holy Shit I Bet You Didn't Know This Volume 2 - I Was Once Blind But Now I See

The Point of No Return

Services Offered by M LeMont

Twitter Consultations and Marketing Services

Jennifer C. Lopez

Beautiful Mind-Spark in Introversion

Thanks, But I'll Teach My Own Kid: A New Generation of Fearless Homeschooler

Spanish Tutorials Online w TheJennieration

Spanish Interpreting and Translation

More Books go MLeMont.com

Resources

This bonus section is for our diehard readers who have read every word and still want more. Google search the headlines.

5 Must Read Articles That Will Inspire You To Greatness.

The Real Reason Books Aren't Finished

JK Rowling "The Fringe Benefits of Failure

Your Elusive Creative Genius | Elizabeth Gilbert

A Deeper Perspective on Co-Authoring

This is Water

http://bulletin.kenyon.edu/x4280.html

M LeMont Acknowledgments

I want to first give thanks to Yahweh the Creator of Heaven and Earth, The Source, Substance, Limits and Bounds of Everything: Thoughts, Experiences, Situations, Desires etc.

It was Yahweh who brought two vessels together; twisting and turning them through time, people, situations, and experiences– down narrow streets and back alleyways–from the coast of Italy to the soft sands of Mexico to find each other for this magnificent project.

Hello, Stranger?

At last we meet.

Jennifer C. Lopez. I could not have written this book without you. You are like sugar to my soul.

Collaborating with the right partner is like getting into a rabbit hole together, and something pulls you deeper and deeper until you become one with each other and then taken to another world filled with amazing thoughts and ideas. A feeling of intimacy that is unexplainable and unsearchable by any physical means.

We WROTE.

We LAUGHED.

We FOUGHT.

We CRIED.

We SURVIVED.

We became as close as two people could become. Nobody will ever know the ADVENTURE we shared.

Thank you Jen, for not quitting. When things got tough–you got tougher.

We made it.

We made it to the top of Mt Everest!

Also, I would like to give thanks to Ted Pindell, my best friend and unreasonable coach who insisted that I co-author this book with Jen and set aside all pride and ego. Thanks for your encouragement and support.

I want to thank my friend of many years Pam Morgan who always shows up when I need her the most. Thanks for your insight, encouragement, and beta reading of the book.

I also want to thank my life-long friend Gene Ward for providing the perfect writing environment. Thanks for your help and the experience. I'm on the other side of that mountain now.

Last, but not least, my daughter Precious– who reads every book her dad has ever written. Thanks honey, for your support. I love you.

Jen's Acknowledgements

Over a year ago, my husband Felipe said to me, "You need to write your book–you have a story."

"YOU are MEANT to WRITE your STORY!"

How little I realized what was to come, when I finally listened.

The sacrifices my husband and daughter Ella made–it never would've happened without them.

¡Gracias mis dos chuletas!

¡Les Amo un chingo!

Mom and Dad: the things you do for your children! You were there to listen, listen and listen some more.

You showed me things I couldn't see for myself, when creating *thejennieration.com* and you did it with the love and enthusiasm only parents could have.

You are the reason I am here. You are a selfless presence and a beacon of hope for me–that there might be others out in the world as good and kind as you!

Ella, mi hija–you are the LIGHT OF MY WORLD and the pure innocent wonder of my every breath. God gave you to me to remind me that the Life is for Loving and that in Love there is always Life. May I teach you one iota of what you have taught me since I had you.

Aunt Dorcas–my angel–thank you for your spiritual support and unyielding love. You are FAMILY.

Gratitude to Joy for always keeping the bond forged.

Holly and Dom–I love you so much!

Last, but not least–M LeMont, you are my Ride & Die writing partner. My "Off-Road" writing experience with you was worth putting my own story aside. We each have our own unique vision–and we found that blending the two would turn into sacrifice and compromise. But together we produced something that represents a shared identity.

You have taught me so much– my gratitude list is long. I will never look at things same way.

Thank you…A forever thank you, for my "Flying Solo to Collaborative" partner.

WH Bone Publishing

Made in the USA
Middletown, DE
11 June 2020

97564219R00248